Razer Blade 16 User Guide

A Comprehensive Step-by-Step Manual
for Setup, Customization,
Troubleshooting, and Advanced
Techniques to Maximize Performance

Oksana Chalifour

1

Disclaimer:

The information contained in this book is intended for general informational purposes only. While every effort has been made to ensure the accuracy and reliability of the content, the author and publisher make no guarantees regarding the accuracy, completeness, or applicability of the information presented.

The Razer Blade 16 User Guide is an independent resource and is not affiliated with, endorsed by, or sponsored by Razer Inc. or any of its subsidiaries. All trademarks, brand names, and product names are the property of their respective owners.

The reader is responsible for following the instructions and recommendations at their own risk. The author and publisher are not liable for any damages, loss of data, or system malfunctions resulting from the use of the information in this book.

Table Of Contents

9

Introduction

The **Razer Blade 16** is not just another laptop—it's a **high-performance machine** built for people who want **power, portability**, and **style**. Whether you're into **gaming, creating content**, or working in a professional capacity, this laptop has the **raw power** to do it all. We're going to walk you through each part of the setup process so that by the end of this guide, you're comfortable using your device.

Overview of Key Features and Specifications

Let's break down the most important features of the **Razer Blade 16** so you can understand **why it's so special** and what makes it stand out.

Mini-LED Display:

- **What's so special about it?** The **Mini-LED display** offers **better contrast**, deeper **blacks**, and more **vibrant colors** compared to traditional LCDs. It's the **perfect screen** for those who need detailed and sharp visuals, whether you're gaming, editing photos, or watching videos.

- **Why does it matter to you?** If you're a gamer, a **4K UHD display** is great for **cinematic visuals**, while **FHD** (Full HD) offers higher refresh rates (up to **144Hz**) for **smoother gameplay**.

- **Tip**: Choose **4K UHD** if you're into media creation or editing, but if you're primarily gaming, **FHD** may be the better choice for **high refresh rates**.

NVIDIA RTX Graphics:

- **What's included?** The **NVIDIA RTX** graphics in the Blade 16 are **top-tier** for **gaming, 3D rendering**, and **content creation**. They support **Ray Tracing**, which simulates realistic lighting and shadows in games and **DLSS**, which improves gaming performance without compromising visual quality.

- **Why does it matter to you?** Ray tracing in games makes **light effects** look more **realistic**, and DLSS helps your games run smoother by **boosting frame rates**.

- **Tip**: You don't need to manually adjust Ray Tracing; most games that support it will automatically turn it on. DLSS can improve performance in demanding games, so it's worth enabling.

Intel Core i9 Processor:

- **What's included?** The **Intel Core i9** processor is one of the **most powerful CPUs** available for laptops. It's designed to handle **heavy multitasking**, demanding **games**, and **content creation software** without breaking a sweat.

- **Why does it matter to you?** Whether you're editing **4K video**, rendering **3D models**, or simply running multiple applications at once, the

13

i9 processor ensures the laptop will **perform seamlessly**.

- **Tip**: This **Core i9 processor** ensures that your laptop can run for **years** without needing an upgrade for performance-related reasons.

Premium Build:

- **What's included?** The **Razer Blade 16** is crafted from **high-quality aluminum** that makes it feel **sturdy** yet **lightweight**.

- **Why does it matter to you?** This design allows you to carry it around with ease without worrying about it being too heavy or fragile. **Professional-looking**, it's perfect for **business meetings** and **creative sessions**.

- **Tip**: The build quality ensures that this laptop **lasts** and can handle the everyday wear-and-tear of being carried in a bag.

Long Battery Life:

- **What's included?** The **Blade 16** is designed with **battery optimization** in mind to balance between **power** and **battery longevity**.

- **Why does it matter to you?** You can expect several hours of use even under heavy tasks like gaming or **video editing**.

- **Tip**: While gaming on battery may reduce the battery life, **balanced power modes** will help you last longer on lighter tasks, like **emailing** or **web browsing**.

Why Choose the Razer Blade 16?

Now that you know about the features, let's talk about **why the Blade 16 is perfect for you**:

For Gamers:

- The **NVIDIA RTX graphics** and **144Hz refresh rate** allow you to play **AAA games** at **smooth frame rates** with **stunning visuals**.

- **Tip for beginners**: If you're a **gamer**, be sure to adjust the settings in **Razer Synapse** to ensure you're running games at the **optimal frame rate**.

For Creators:

- Whether you're editing **photos**, **videos**, or creating **3D models**, the **Blade 16** offers the **processing power** and **accurate display** that professionals need.

- **Tip for beginners**: To take full advantage of the display, adjust the **color calibration** settings and use software like **Adobe Premiere Pro** or **DaVinci Resolve** for video editing.

For Business Professionals:

- The **Blade 16's performance** will handle demanding **business tasks**, such as running **virtual meetings**, managing **large datasets**, and multitasking.

- **Tip for beginners**: Install essential business applications, such as **Microsoft Office**, and use

cloud storage like **OneDrive** for seamless file management.

What Makes the Razer Blade 16 Stand Out in the Market?

Premium Design:

- Unlike many bulky gaming laptops, the **Blade 16** has a **sleek, slim design** without compromising on **power**.

- **Tip**: Enjoy portability while still benefiting from **desktop-like performance**.

Customization:

- **Razer Synapse** allows you to **customize RGB lighting**, adjust **fan speeds**, and **optimize performance profiles** for various tasks.

- **Tip for beginners**: Install **Razer Synapse** to get the most out of the RGB lighting and manage your system performance to suit your needs.

Upgradeable Components:

- The **RAM** and **storage** can be easily upgraded, ensuring the **Blade 16** remains capable as software requirements grow.

- **Tip for beginners**: Don't worry if you run out of storage—just buy a new **SSD** or add more **RAM** as needed.

Cooling System:

- Despite the powerful components, the **Blade 16** stays **cool** under load due to its advanced cooling system.

- **Tip for beginners**: You can adjust the fan speed using **Razer Synapse** if you want a quieter experience while working or gaming.

Future-Proofing Your Device: Understanding Blade 16's Longevity

Upgradeable RAM and Storage:

- You can **easily upgrade** the **RAM** and **storage** in the future to meet **growing needs**. This means you won't have to replace the laptop when you need more power.

- **Tip for beginners**: If you start running low on space or need more memory, check the **storage** options in the laptop's **settings** to see what can be upgraded.

Processor and Graphics:

- The **Intel Core i9 processor** and **NVIDIA RTX graphics** ensure that the Blade 16 can handle **new software**, **games**, and **tasks** for years to come.

- **Tip for beginners**: You're unlikely to need an upgrade for the **GPU** or **CPU** for at least 3-4 years.

Long-Term Support:

- Razer provides **continuous updates**, so your laptop will stay current with new features, bug fixes, and security patches.

- **Tip for beginners**: Always make sure your laptop is set to **automatically update** to avoid missing important updates.

How to Use This Guide

This guide is designed to help **beginners** set up and use their **Razer Blade 16** with ease. It's structured in a **step-by-step** manner, so you can follow along without any confusion.

A Beginner's Walkthrough of the Guide

- **Step 1**: Start with the **Getting Started** chapter, where we'll guide you through the process of **unboxing** and **setting up** your laptop.

- **Step 2**: Once set up, move on to the **Design and Components** chapter to learn about the **physical features** and key components of your new laptop.

- **Step 3**: Afterward, check out the **Maximizing Performance** chapter to see how you can get the **best performance** for gaming, work, or media creation.

How to Navigate and Find the Information You Need

This guide is organized into chapters, each covering a specific aspect of using your **Razer Blade 16**. Here's how to use it:

1. **Getting Started**: Learn how to **unbox** and **set up** your Blade 16, configure **Windows 11**, and make sure your laptop is ready for use.

2. **Design and Components**: Understand the layout of the **keyboard, ports**, and the **Mini-LED display**.

3. **Gaming Performance**: Discover tips and settings for **optimizing gaming performance**.

4. **Content Creation**: Learn how to **optimize settings** for video and photo editing.

5. **Business Productivity**: Set up the Blade 16 for **work** tasks and learn how to manage **files** and **apps**.

6. **Troubleshooting and Maintenance**: Solve common issues and learn how to **maintain** your Blade 16 over time.

You can navigate the guide by using the **Table of Contents**, which lists all the chapters. This way, you can jump to the chapter that best fits your current needs.

Quick Start for New Users: Key Sections to Focus On

If you're **just getting started** with your **Razer Blade 16**:

1. **Start with Chapter 1: Getting Started** to set up your device and ensure everything is properly configured.

2. **Move to Chapter 2: Design and Components** to familiarize yourself with the hardware.

3. As you get more comfortable, explore the chapters on **gaming, performance,** and **troubleshooting**.

Unboxing the Razer Blade 16

What's Included in the Box?

When you open your **Razer Blade 16** box, you should see:

1. **Razer Blade 16 Laptop**

2. **Power Adapter** (230W or 330W)

3. **Quick Start Guide** to walk you through the initial setup

4. **Warranty and Safety Information**

5. **Razer Stickers** (for personalization)

First Impressions and Key Features Overview

- **Build Quality**: The Blade 16 feels **premium** thanks to its **aluminum unibody**. It's lightweight but sturdy.

- **Display**: The **Mini-LED** screen offers **vivid colors** and sharp details, making it great for gaming and content creation.

- **Keyboard**: The **RGB lighting** is customizable, adding a personal touch.

Setting Up Your Laptop for the First Time

1. **Unbox the Blade 16**: Take it out of the box carefully, ensuring you have all the items listed.

2. **Plug in the Charger**: Connect the **power adapter** to the laptop and an **electrical outlet**.

3. **Power On the Device**: Press the **power button** on the top-right corner of the keyboard.

4. **Windows 11 Setup**:

   o Choose your **language** and **region**.

   o Connect to your **Wi-Fi network** and sign in to your **Microsoft account**.

   o **Set up Windows Hello**, which will allow you to sign in using a **PIN** or **fingerprint**.

Your **Razer Blade 16** is now ready to use!

Congratulations! You've successfully **unboxed** and **set up** your **Razer Blade 16**. This guide has helped you understand the device's features and walked you through the **setup process**. Now, you're ready to dive into **gaming**, **content creation**, or **work** with confidence!

Chapter 1

Getting Started

Powering Up Your Razer Blade 16

Turning on Your Laptop for the Very First Time

Unbox Your Laptop

When you first open the box, remove the **Razer Blade 16** carefully. Inside, you should find:

- The **laptop** itself, which is the main device.

- The **power adapter** (this is the charger for your laptop).

- The **power cable** (this connects the charger to the wall outlet).

- A **quick start guide** (this is a manual to help you get started).

- **Warranty information** (this tells you about the warranty for your laptop).

- **Razer stickers** (fun extras you can use to customize your laptop).

- **Tip for beginners**: Make sure everything is in place and undamaged before moving forward. It's easy to overlook things when unboxing, but checking all items ensures nothing is missing.

Plugging in the Power Adapter

- Before turning your laptop on, plug in the **power adapter** to make sure it has enough power for the setup process.

- Find the **charging port** on the left or back side of the laptop (this is where the power adapter connects). Insert the **smaller end** of the **power adapter** into this port.

- Take the **larger end** of the power cable and plug it into a **wall outlet** or **surge protector** (this helps protect your laptop from power surges).

- **Tip for beginners**: It's important to ensure the **power cable** is plugged in securely to avoid running out of battery during the setup process.

Powering On the Laptop

- Once the laptop is plugged in, you'll need to **turn it on**.

- Locate the **power button** on your laptop, typically at the **top-right corner** of the keyboard.

- **Press and hold** the power button for **2-3 seconds** until you see the **Razer logo** appear on the screen. This indicates the laptop is **starting up**.

- **Tip for beginners**: If the screen doesn't turn on, double-check the power cable connection and ensure it's properly plugged in.

Setting Up Windows 11 and Account Configuration

Now that your laptop is powered on, it's time to set up **Windows 11**. This is the operating system that runs your **Razer Blade 16**, and during the setup, you'll configure basic things like language, region, and your user account.

Choosing Your Language

- When you first turn on the laptop, Windows will ask you to select your **preferred language** for the system. You will see a list of languages such as **English**, **Spanish**, and others.

- **Use the trackpad** to select the language you want and click **Next**.

- **Tip for beginners**: If you are unsure about the language, **English** is a safe and universal choice.

Select Your Region

- The next screen will ask you to choose your **region** (this is your country).

- For example, if you live in the **United States**, choose **United States** from the list and click **Next**.

- **Tip for beginners**: It's important to select the correct region because this will ensure that **time zones**, **currency**, and **date formats** are set correctly for your location.

Connecting to Wi-Fi

- Windows will prompt you to connect your laptop to a **Wi-Fi network**.

- A list of **available networks** will appear. Select the **network** you want to connect to, then enter the **password** and click **Connect**.

- **Tip for beginners**: If you don't have Wi-Fi available, you can skip this step and connect to Wi-Fi later. However, it's a good idea to connect now so **Windows 11** can automatically download updates and configure your system.

Sign in to Your Microsoft Account

- Next, Windows will ask you to **sign in to a Microsoft account**.

- If you already have a Microsoft account (like an **Outlook** or **Hotmail** email), enter your **email** and **password** to sign in.

- If you don't have a Microsoft account, you can easily create one by selecting **Create one** and following the on-screen instructions.

- Alternatively, you can select **Offline Account** for a simpler login process without syncing with Microsoft services.

- **Tip for beginners**: A **Microsoft account** is useful because it allows you to **sync settings**, **access cloud storage (OneDrive)**, and download apps from the **Microsoft Store**. But using a **local account** is perfectly fine if you don't want to sign in.

Configure Privacy Settings

- Windows will ask for your **privacy preferences**, such as whether to share **diagnostic data** with Microsoft and whether you want to enable location services.

- **Tip for beginners**: You can choose **Recommended settings** to automatically balance privacy and functionality. These settings are safe, but you can change them later in the **Privacy settings** section if needed.

Finalizing Setup

- Once you've confirmed your settings, Windows will finish the **setup process**. This may take a few minutes, so sit back and relax while your laptop prepares for use.

- **Tip for beginners**: This setup might take longer if your laptop needs to download updates. Let the process run until it's complete.

Connecting to Wi-Fi and Bluetooth for the First Time

Wi-Fi Connection

- If you skipped the Wi-Fi setup earlier, now is a good time to connect.

- Go to **Settings → Network & Internet → Wi-Fi**, and select your desired Wi-Fi network.

- Enter your **Wi-Fi password** and connect.

- **Tip for beginners**: Ensure you type the **Wi-Fi password** correctly. It's **case-sensitive**, so check that every letter is in the correct case.

Bluetooth Setup

- If you use **Bluetooth** devices (e.g., **wireless headphones, Bluetooth speakers**, or a **wireless mouse**), you can enable **Bluetooth** in **Settings** → **Devices** → **Bluetooth & other devices**.

- Turn the **Bluetooth toggle** to **On**, and then you can begin pairing your Bluetooth devices.

- **Tip for beginners**: You can skip this step if you don't use Bluetooth, but it's easy to enable later by following the same steps.

First-Time Setup: Configuring Windows 11

Personalizing Your Desktop (Themes, Wallpaper, Lock Screen)

Change Your Desktop Background

- Right-click on an empty area of your **desktop** and select **Personalize** from the menu.

- In the **Background** section, you can select a **picture, solid color,** or **slideshow**. You can also click **Browse** to choose a custom image from your **Pictures folder**.

- **Tip for beginners**: Choose a default **image** for now if you don't have a custom one, or pick a **solid color** to keep it simple.

Set Your Lock Screen

- Under **Lock Screen** settings, you can select an image for the screen that appears when your laptop is **locked**.

- You can choose **Windows Spotlight** for daily changing images, or select a **pre-set photo**.

- **Tip for beginners**: Choose **Windows Spotlight** for dynamic lock screen images that change each day.

Select Your Theme

- Go to **Themes** and select either a **light theme** (bright interface) or a **dark theme** (dark interface).

- **Tip for beginners**: **Dark mode** is easier on the eyes, especially when using your laptop at night or in low-light environments.

Setting Up Windows 11 Features (Cortana, Widgets, Virtual Desktops)

Cortana Setup

- **Cortana** is Windows' voice assistant, similar to **Siri** or **Google Assistant**. It helps you with things like setting **reminders**, answering questions, and opening apps.

- You can enable **Cortana** or skip it if you don't need it.

- **Tip for beginners**: If you're unsure, feel free to skip Cortana for now. You can always turn it on later.

Widgets

- **Widgets** are small information boxes that show updates such as **weather**, **news**, and **calendar** events.

- You can access widgets by clicking the **Widgets icon** on the taskbar.

- **Tip for beginners**: If you find widgets unnecessary, you can disable them by right-clicking the **taskbar** and turning off **Widgets**.

Virtual Desktops

- **Virtual Desktops** let you create separate **desktops** for different activities. For instance, you can create one desktop for **work** and another for **gaming**.

- To create a new desktop, press **Win + Tab** and click **New Desktop**.

- **Tip for beginners**: Stick with one desktop for now. You can experiment with multiple desktops as you get more comfortable.

Configuring Privacy and Security Settings (Windows Hello, PIN, Fingerprint)

Windows Hello

- **Windows Hello** allows you to log in using **Face Recognition**, **Fingerprint**, or a **PIN**. These methods are faster and more secure than using a traditional password.

- Go to **Settings** → **Accounts** → **Sign-in options** to set up **Windows Hello**.

- **Tip for beginners**: The easiest option is **PIN**, but you can set up **Face Recognition** or **Fingerprint** for added security if your laptop supports it.

Windows Security (Windows Defender)

- **Windows Defender** is built into Windows 11 and helps protect your laptop from **viruses** and **malware**. It runs in the background, so you don't have to manually enable it.

- **Tip for beginners**: Don't worry about **Windows Defender**—it's automatically activated and protects your laptop from threats.

Battery Management and Charging

Charging the Razer Blade 16 for the First Time

First Charge

- Once you've completed the setup, it's important to **fully charge** your laptop for **optimal battery health**. Plug the **power adapter** into the laptop and let it charge until it reaches **100%**.

- **Tip for beginners**: Let the laptop charge completely the first time to help **calibrate** the battery.

Battery Life Expectations and Optimizing Power Settings

Battery Life

- On lighter tasks, such as **web browsing** and **document editing**, the battery should last about **6-8 hours**.

- For more intensive tasks, such as **gaming** or **video editing**, the battery will drain faster, around **2-4 hours**.

- **Tip for beginners**: Keep an eye on battery life during heavy tasks and plug in the laptop when needed.

Optimizing Power Settings

- Go to **Settings** → **System** → **Power & Battery** to adjust **power settings**.

- **Power Saver** extends battery life, while **Best Performance** maximizes power for demanding applications.

- **Tip for beginners**: Use **Balanced Mode** for everyday tasks, and switch to **Best Performance** for gaming or when running resource-intensive programs.

How to Use Power Modes for Maximum Battery Life vs. Performance

Switching Power Modes

- Windows 11 allows you to adjust your power usage:

  o **Power Saver** for extended battery life.

  o **Balanced** for regular use.

  o **Best Performance** for demanding tasks like **gaming**.

- **Tip for beginners**: Use **Balanced** for regular tasks. Only switch to **Best Performance** when running demanding applications, and use **Power Saver** when you need your laptop to last longer without charging.

Now that you've completed the **setup process** for your **Razer Blade 16**, you're ready to enjoy all the **powerful features** this laptop has to offer! You've personalized your **desktop**, set up **Wi-Fi**, and configured **privacy** and **security** settings. Your laptop is fully prepared for **gaming**, **content creation**, or **productivity**.

Chapter 2

Understanding the Razer Blade 16 Design and Components

This chapter will break down the **physical components**, **display settings**, **cooling systems**, and **sound settings** of your **Razer Blade 16**. It will teach you exactly how to use each part, step by step, to get the best performance and visual/audio experience from your laptop.

Overview of the Razer Blade 16 Design

The **Razer Blade 16** is a powerful gaming laptop built for **high performance** and **portability**. Let's get familiar with the components.

Physical Layout and Key Components of the Blade 16

Laptop Body:

- The **Razer Blade 16** has a **premium aluminum body** that makes it both **lightweight** and **durable**. This design helps keep it **cool** during use, as aluminum can dissipate heat effectively.

- **How to use it**: When you first pick up the laptop, you'll feel the **smooth, cool surface**. If you're traveling or carrying it in a bag, make sure not to put pressure on the screen or keyboard to prevent any damage.

The Display:

- The **Mini-LED display** of the **Razer Blade 16** is one of the most advanced screens on a laptop. It offers **brighter colors, deeper blacks,** and **greater contrast** than traditional LED screens, and it supports **HDR (High Dynamic Range)** for vibrant visuals.

- **How to use it**: To get the best experience, you'll want to **adjust the screen brightness**. This can be done quickly using the **keyboard shortcut** (usually **F5** to decrease brightness and **F6** to increase brightness) or by going into **Settings** → **System** → **Display** and adjusting the brightness slider.

Tip for beginners: If you're in a **bright environment**, increase the brightness so that you can see the screen clearly. In **low-light environments**, you can lower it to save battery.

The Keyboard and Trackpad:

- The **keyboard** is **RGB backlit**, meaning it lights up in different colors, and you can customize this. The **trackpad** is large and responsive, making it easier to navigate through tasks when you're not using an external mouse.

- **How to use it**:

  - **Keyboard**: Use the **arrow keys** to navigate through menus and select items,

34

the **Enter key** to confirm selections, and the **Spacebar** for scrolling or jumping in and out of options.

o **Trackpad**: Use **one finger** to **move the cursor** on the screen. **Two fingers** allow you to **scroll** through documents or web pages, and **three fingers** can help you switch between virtual desktops or open apps on **Windows 11**.

o To adjust the **backlight color** of your keyboard, download the **Razer Synapse software** and follow the instructions to set up lighting effects.

Ports and Connectivity Overview (USB-C, HDMI, Thunderbolt, etc.)

Understanding the **ports** on your laptop is crucial for connecting to external devices, whether it's for **charging**, **external displays**, or **audio equipment**. Let's go step by step on how to use each of the **Razer Blade 16's** ports.

USB-C Ports:

• The **USB-C ports** are used to connect modern devices such as **external storage drives**, **monitors**, and even **external GPUs**. One of these ports supports **Thunderbolt 4**, which provides **super-fast data transfer speeds**.

• **How to use it**: To connect a **USB-C device**, simply insert the **USB-C cable** into one of the **USB-C ports**. If you're using a **Thunderbolt-**

compatible device, it can be plugged into the **Thunderbolt 4 port** for **faster data transfer**.

HDMI Port:

- The **HDMI port** is used to connect to **external monitors** or **TVs**, making it perfect for extending your display to a bigger screen.

- **How to use it**: To connect an **HDMI monitor**:

  o Plug one end of an **HDMI cable** into the **HDMI port** on your laptop.

  o Connect the other end to the **HDMI input** on your **monitor** or **TV**.

  o Once connected, go to **Settings** → **System** → **Display** and choose how you want to use the second screen (either to extend your display or duplicate it).

USB-A Ports:

- These are the **traditional USB ports** (rectangular-shaped), and they are still widely used for **flash drives**, **external mice**, or **keyboards**.

- **How to use it**: Simply plug the **USB-A device** (e.g., a **mouse** or **keyboard**) into the **USB-A port**, and it should automatically be recognized by the system.

3.5mm Headphone Jack:

- The **3.5mm headphone jack** is used to plug in **wired headphones** or **external speakers**.

- **How to use it**: Plug the **headphone jack** into the **port** on the laptop and you'll be able to hear sound from your **headphones** or **speakers**.

Power Input:

- The **power input** port is where you connect the **charging cable**.

- **How to use it**: Insert the **charging cable** into the **charging port** and connect the **other end** to a **wall outlet** to start charging.

The Keyboard and Trackpad: Features and Customizations

The **keyboard** and **trackpad** are two of the most used components on your laptop, so let's break down exactly how to get the most out of them.

Keyboard Features:

- The **keyboard** has **RGB backlighting** that you can customize using **Razer Synapse** software.

- **How to use it**:

  - To adjust the **keyboard lighting**, press **FN + F11** to decrease brightness, or **FN + F12** to increase it.

  - To **customize lighting** or set it to a **dynamic color profile**, open **Razer Synapse**, navigate to **Chroma Studio**, and select your desired effects.

Trackpad:

- The **trackpad** is **large** and **responsive**. It allows you to move the cursor, scroll, and click using simple gestures.

- **How to use it**:
  - **One-finger**: Moves the cursor around the screen.

  - **Two-fingers**: Scrolls up/down or left/right through documents or web pages.

  - **Three-fingers**: Swipes between **virtual desktops** or **opens multitasking view** on **Windows 11**.

  - To **adjust the trackpad settings** (like sensitivity), go to **Settings → Devices → Touchpad** and make changes as needed.

Display Settings

Now, let's talk about how to make sure your **Mini-LED display** is set up properly to get the best visual experience for **gaming**, **creative work**, or **daily tasks**.

Mini-LED Technology: Resolution, Color Accuracy, and HDR

Mini-LED Technology:

- **Mini-LED** offers **better contrast** and **color accuracy** than traditional LED displays. It's perfect for watching **HDR movies**, **gaming**, or working on **photo editing**.

- **How to use it**: The **Mini-LED** technology is built into the screen and automatically works once you turn the laptop on. You don't need to make any special adjustments to activate it, but make sure to adjust the **brightness** based on your environment.

HDR Support:

- **HDR (High Dynamic Range)** provides more vibrant colors and brighter whites for a **better viewing experience**.

- **How to use it**: If you're watching **HDR content** (such as **HDR-enabled movies** or **games**), make sure **HDR** is enabled in the **Display settings**. Go to **Settings** → **System** → **Display** and check the **HDR** setting.

Choosing Between 4K UHD vs FHD for Specific Use Cases (Gaming, Editing, etc.)

4K UHD Display:

- The **4K UHD** resolution (3840 x 2160) offers **crisp details** for **creative tasks** like **photo editing** or **video production**.

- **How to use it**: Select **4K resolution** from **Display settings** if you're editing media or need ultra-high detail. Keep in mind, using **4K** will consume more **battery**.

FHD Display:

- The **Full HD (FHD)** resolution (1920 x 1080) is ideal for **gaming**, **video streaming**, or general use.

- **How to use it**: If you're a **gamer, FHD** is often better as it allows for smoother performance with higher **frame rates**.

Adjusting Display Settings for Optimal Gaming and Creative Work

Resolution Adjustment:

- **How to do it**: To adjust the **resolution**, go to Settings → **System** → **Display** → **Display Resolution**. Here, select **FHD (1920 x 1080)** or **4K UHD (3840 x 2160)** based on your needs.

Refresh Rate Adjustment:

- **How to do it**: For **smooth gaming** performance, you should use a higher **refresh rate** (e.g., **120Hz** or **165Hz**). To change it, go to **Settings** → **System** → **Display** → **Advanced Display Settings** and select the desired refresh rate.

Cooling System and Thermal Management

To keep your **Razer Blade 16** cool and running smoothly, here's how the **cooling system** works.

How the Blade 16's Cooling System Works: Vapor Chamber and Fan Profiles

Vapor Chamber:

- The **vapor chamber** helps evenly distribute **heat** across the laptop, ensuring the system stays cool even when performing demanding tasks.

- **Tip for beginners**: You don't need to adjust the **cooling system** manually. The **vapor chamber** automatically helps dissipate heat during use, especially under load.

Configuring Razer Synapse for Cooling and Thermal Profiles

How to do it: To change the **cooling profile**:

- Open **Razer Synapse**, go to **Performance** settings, and select from **Balanced**, **Performance**, or **Quiet Mode**.

- **Tip for beginners**: Select **Performance Mode** for **gaming** or **resource-heavy tasks**. Use **Quiet Mode** for general tasks when you want to reduce fan noise.

Sound System and Audio Settings

Now, let's adjust the **audio settings** for the best sound experience, whether you're gaming, watching movies, or listening to music.

Configuring Audio Settings for Gaming and Media Consumption

Adjusting Volume:

- To change the **volume**, use the **volume buttons** on your keyboard or click the **speaker icon** on the

taskbar. From there, adjust the slider to increase or decrease the sound.

Changing Output Devices:

- If you're using **external speakers** or **headphones**, go to **Settings** → **System** → **Sound**, and select your output device (such as **headphones** or **speakers**).

Using Dolby Atmos for Enhanced Audio

Enable Dolby Atmos:

- To get **3D surround sound**, go to **Settings** → **Sound** → **Spatial Sound** and select **Dolby Atmos**.

- **Tip for beginners: Dolby Atmos** works best with **headphones**, providing a more immersive experience, especially for **games** or **movies**.

You now have a thorough understanding of the **Razer Blade 16's components, display settings, cooling system**, and **audio settings**. Whether you're into **gaming, creative work**, or **media consumption**, you now know how to customize your **Razer Blade 16** for the best experience possible.

By following these **step-by-step instructions**, you'll be able to use your laptop to its fullest potential—whether you're adjusting your **keyboard lighting**, fine-tuning your **screen resolution**, or managing the **cooling system** for high-performance tasks.

Chapter 3

Maximizing Performance with Razer Synapse

Razer Synapse is a powerful software that allows you to **customize** and **optimize** your **Razer Blade 16**. It gives you complete control over features like **RGB lighting**, **performance settings**, and even **cooling management**, allowing you to tailor the laptop's behavior based on your specific needs, whether it's for **gaming**, **work**, or **entertainment**.

What is Razer Synapse?

Razer Synapse is the **central hub** for managing all the settings related to your **Razer Blade 16**'s **customization**. It allows you to adjust **RGB lighting**, **performance modes**, **cooling**, and **macros** for a personalized experience. Let's walk you through **what it is** and **how to install and use it**.

Introduction to Razer Synapse Software for Customization

What is Razer Synapse?

- **Razer Synapse** is a **software suite** developed by **Razer** that enables you to customize various aspects of your **Razer Blade 16**.

- This software controls:

- o **RGB lighting customization** for your keyboard and connected devices (through **Razer Chroma**).

- o **Performance settings** that can be adjusted for tasks like **gaming, work**, or **battery saving**.

- o **Cooling profiles** to prevent your laptop from overheating during **gaming** or **video rendering**.

- o **Key remapping and macro creation** to enhance your **gaming or productivity** workflows.

Installing and Setting Up Razer Synapse on Your Blade 16

Download Razer Synapse:

- Go to the **Razer website** on your **laptop**'s browser: www.razer.com.

- Navigate to **Support** and click on **Downloads**.

- Find the **Razer Synapse** section and click on the **Windows** version to start downloading the installer.

Install the Software:

- After downloading, go to your **downloads folder** and open the **installer file**.

- Click **Install**, and the software will begin to install on your **Razer Blade 16**.

- Once installation is complete, you can open **Razer Synapse** either from the **desktop shortcut** or by searching for it in the **Start menu**.

Create or Log into Your Razer Account:

- After opening **Razer Synapse**, you will be asked to **log in** or **create an account**. If you don't have an account, click on **Create Account** and follow the steps.

- **Tip for beginners**: You can link your **Google** or **Facebook** accounts to sign in faster.

Device Detection:

- Once logged in, **Razer Synapse** will automatically detect your **Razer Blade 16** and begin applying the default settings.

RGB Lighting Customization with Razer Chroma

Razer Synapse provides powerful customization of the **RGB lighting** through **Razer Chroma**. Here's how you can make your laptop visually unique and sync the lighting with your **gaming** or **workflow needs**.

Creating and Syncing Custom Lighting Profiles for Gaming, Work, and Media

Open Razer Synapse:

- Launch **Razer Synapse** from your **Start menu** or **desktop shortcut**.

- In the main interface, navigate to the **Chroma Studio** tab to start customizing your lighting.

Creating a New Profile:

- Click on **Create New Profile** at the top of the screen.

- Name your profile based on the activity (e.g., **Gaming**, **Work**, **Media**).

- This will allow you to set up specific lighting settings for different activities.

Customize Key Colors:

- In the **Chroma Studio**, you'll see a virtual representation of your **keyboard**.

- Click on a **key** you want to change, then select a **color** for that key from the **color wheel** or choose from preset **color options** (e.g., red, blue, green).

- **Tip for beginners**: You can color-code your **WASD keys** in a different color for **gaming** and leave the rest of the keys a neutral color for **work**.

Add Lighting Effects:

- **Chroma Studio** allows you to add different lighting effects, such as:
    - **Static**: A fixed color across all keys.
    - **Breathing**: The lights will gradually brighten and dim, like **breathing**.
    - **Reactive**: The keys light up when pressed.

○ **Wave**: The lights move across the keyboard in a wave pattern.

- Select an effect from the **Effect** dropdown, and adjust the **speed** and **direction** of the effect.

Sync Lighting with Games:

- Some **games** support **Chroma integration**, meaning the lighting will change based on **game events** (e.g., **health** or **abilities**).

- To sync your lighting, go to the **Chroma Studio** and find the **Game Integration** section. Here, selects your game (e.g., **Fortnite, Cyberpunk 2077**).

- **Tip for beginners**: If you play a game that supports **Chroma** integration, enable it to make your lighting react dynamically.

Using Chroma Studio to Customize Key Colors, Effects, and Animations

Animating the Lighting:

- In **Chroma Studio**, you can also adjust the **speed** of animations (such as the **Wave** effect).

- Click on the **Animation** tab, select the effect you want, and adjust its speed and direction.

Save and Apply Your Profile:

- Once you're happy with your lighting, click **Save** at the bottom.

- To switch between different profiles (e.g., **Gaming**, **Work**), go to the **Profiles** tab in **Chroma Studio**, and click on the profile you want to use.

Performance Tuning and Cooling Management

In **Razer Synapse**, you can customize your laptop's **performance** and **cooling profiles**. These settings can significantly affect how your laptop operates depending on your current activity—whether you're **gaming**, **video editing**, or **working**.

Using Razer Synapse to Adjust Performance Modes (Balanced, Performance, Battery)

Open Razer Synapse and navigate to the **Performance** tab.

You will see options for **Balanced**, **Performance**, and **Battery** modes.

1. **Balanced Mode**: This mode gives you a **good mix** of **performance** and **battery life**. It's ideal for regular tasks like **web browsing**, **office work**, or **media consumption**.

2. **Performance Mode**: This mode maximizes your laptop's **performance** by increasing the power to the **CPU** and **GPU**, making it great for **gaming** or **video rendering**.

3. **Battery Mode**: This mode reduces **power consumption** to extend battery life. It's useful when you're **not near a charger**.

How to switch modes:

- Click on the mode you want to use (e.g., **Performance Mode**) based on your current task.

Tip for beginners: Use **Performance Mode** for gaming or **intensive tasks** that require high performance, and use **Battery Mode** when you need the laptop to last longer on a single charge.

Cooling Profiles for Optimal Heat Management During Gaming or Editing

Adjusting Cooling Profiles:

- Your **Razer Blade 16** has **three cooling profiles** to choose from:

    o **Balanced**: Offers a balance between cooling and noise.

    o **Performance**: Maximizes cooling for **intensive tasks** like **gaming** or **video editing**.

    o **Quiet**: Minimizes fan noise for tasks that don't generate much heat.

- **How to adjust cooling profiles**:

Go to the **Cooling** tab in **Razer Synapse**.

Select the cooling profile that matches your current task.

Advanced Cooling Settings:

- For even more control, you can adjust **fan speeds** manually and optimize how your laptop handles heat under load.

Advanced GPU/CPU Power Settings and Thermal Management via Synapse

Adjusting GPU and CPU Power Settings:

- Under the **Performance** tab in **Razer Synapse**, you can customize how much power is dedicated to the **CPU** and **GPU** during demanding tasks like **gaming** or **rendering**.

- **How to do it**:

  o In **Razer Synapse**, go to **Advanced Settings** in the **Performance** tab.

  o Adjust the **power settings** for your **GPU** and **CPU**.

  o Increase power to the **GPU** for gaming or decrease it when you need to save battery.

Tip for beginners: If you're gaming, increase the **GPU power** for higher frame rates. For regular work, reduce the power to extend battery life.

Game-Specific Profiles and User-Centric Customization

One of the great features of **Razer Synapse** is its ability to automatically apply **performance profiles** based on the game you're playing. This ensures your laptop is always optimized for gaming or productivity.

Automatically Applying Performance Profiles Based on Game Title

Setting Up Game-Specific Profiles:

- **Razer Synapse** lets you create **game-specific profiles** that automatically apply **performance settings** when you launch the game.

- **How to set it up**:

    o Go to **Razer Synapse** and navigate to **Game Profiles**.

    o Click **Create New Profile** and name it after the game (e.g., **Fortnite, Call of Duty**).

    o Adjust the **performance**, **lighting**, and **cooling** settings for that specific game.

Saving and Applying:

- When you open the game, **Razer Synapse** will automatically switch to the profile you created, ensuring your laptop runs at **optimal performance** for that specific game.

Customizing Keyboard Shortcuts, Key Remapping, and Macro Settings

Creating Macros:

- **Macros** are a series of keypresses or actions that can be executed with a single button.

- **How to set up**:
  - Open **Razer Synapse** and go to the **Macro** tab.
  - Click **Create New Macro** and start recording your actions (key presses, mouse clicks).
  - Assign the macro to a key on your keyboard.

Key Remapping:

- If you want to assign a specific function to a different key (for example, remapping the **F1 key** to open **your favorite website**), you can do so within **Razer Synapse**.

- **How to do it**:
  - Go to **Keyboard** settings in **Razer Synapse**.
  - Click on the key you want to remap, then choose a new function or macro from the options.

By following these detailed steps, you now know how to use **Razer Synapse** to customize your **Razer Blade 16** for different tasks. Whether you're **gaming**, **working**, or **watching media**, you can adjust the **lighting**, **performance**, **cooling**, and **macros** to suit your needs.

Chapter 4

Maximizing Gaming Performance

This chapter will teach you how to get the best **gaming experience** on your **Razer Blade 16**. Whether you're new to gaming or looking to enhance your gaming setup, this guide will take you through everything you need to do to **optimize your system** for the best performance, visuals, and overall experience.

Configuring Your Gaming Setup for Maximum Performance

Your **gaming setup** plays a crucial role in how your games run. Let's walk through how to install **game clients**, enable **Game Mode**, and tweak **performance settings** for the best gaming experience.

Installing and Managing Game Clients (Steam, Epic Games Store, etc.)

To start gaming, you'll need to install **game clients**. These platforms allow you to download, manage, and launch games.

Steam:

- **How to install**:
    - Open a browser and go to the **Steam website** (steam.com).

- o Click **Install Steam** at the top of the page.

- o Follow the on-screen instructions to download and install the **Steam client**.

- o Once installed, open **Steam**, sign in or create a new account, and browse the **Steam store** to purchase or download your games.

- **Tip for beginners**: Once you have **Steam installed**, you can manage all your games through the **library**, and it will automatically keep them updated.

Epic Games Store:

- **How to install**:

  - o Go to the **Epic Games Store website** (epicgames.com).

  - o Click on **Get Epic Games** to download the Epic Games Launcher.

  - o Once the installer is downloaded, open it and follow the instructions to install the launcher.

  - o After installation, sign in or create an account, then browse for games and install them.

- **Tip for beginners**: Like Steam, **Epic Games Store** also offers **free games** regularly, so check it often.

Game Mode vs Performance Mode: Understanding Performance Settings

Both **Game Mode** and **Performance Mode** are designed to optimize your system's performance for gaming, but they do so in slightly different ways.

Game Mode:

- **What it does**: **Game Mode** prioritizes your system's resources for gaming. It reduces background processes and helps boost frame rates by focusing resources on the game itself.

- **How to enable it**:

  - Press **Windows Key + G** to bring up the **Game Bar**.

  - Click on **Settings** (the gear icon) in the Game Bar.

  - In the settings menu, toggle **Game Mode** to **On**.

  - You can also enable **Game Mode** through **Windows Settings** → **Gaming** → **Game Mode**.

Performance Mode:

- **What it does**: **Performance Mode** ensures that the laptop runs at its highest possible speed by allowing the **CPU** and **GPU** to reach full performance, especially during **gaming** or **resource-heavy tasks**.

- **How to enable it**:

    o Open **Razer Synapse**.

    o Navigate to **Performance** → **Battery**.

    o Select **Performance Mode** for gaming and high-performance tasks.

- **Tip for beginners**: Use **Game Mode** if you're focused on gaming and want better frame rates, but use **Performance Mode** for sustained, high-performance activities like **video rendering**.

Optimizing Game-Specific Settings for GPU/CPU Performance

To get the best performance in your games, you need to tweak the settings in both **Razer Synapse** and the **game clients**.

In Steam or Epic Games Store:

- **How to do it**:

    o Open your game from **Steam** or **Epic Games Store**.

    o Go to **Settings** or **Options** within the game's menu.

    o Set the **resolution** to match your **display** (e.g., **FHD** or **4K**).

    o Enable settings like **V-Sync**, **Anti-Aliasing**, and **Texture Quality** for better visuals, but keep in mind that higher settings may lower frame rates.

In Razer Synapse:

- **How to do it:**

    o Open **Razer Synapse**.

    o Go to **Performance** → **GPU Settings**.

    o Set the **performance** mode to **Maximum** for demanding games.

    o Adjust **cooling profiles** to ensure that your laptop stays cool while running games.

Optimizing GPU and Visual Quality for Gaming

The **NVIDIA RTX GPU** on the **Razer Blade 16** offers cutting-edge features that greatly enhance gaming visuals and performance.

Understanding NVIDIA RTX 40-Series Graphics Features (Ray Tracing, DLSS)

Ray Tracing:

- **What it is**: Ray tracing simulates the way light interacts with objects in the real world. This creates more realistic **lighting**, **shadows**, and **reflections** in supported games.

- **How to enable it:**

- Open your game and go to **Settings** → **Graphics** or **Visual Settings**.

- Look for **Ray Tracing** and turn it **On**.

- Ray tracing may impact frame rates, so you may need to balance this setting with other visual effects.

DLSS (Deep Learning Super Sampling):

- **What it is: DLSS** is a technology by **NVIDIA** that uses **AI** to upscale lower-resolution images to **higher resolutions**. This helps improve **frame rates** without sacrificing visual quality.

- **How to enable it:**

  - In your game settings, find the **DLSS** option.

  - Set it to **Quality** for the best balance of visuals and performance.

  - **DLSS** should automatically optimize game performance, especially in **GPU-intensive games**.

Configuring NVIDIA Control Panel for Gaming Graphics and Performance

Open NVIDIA Control Panel:

- Right-click on the **desktop** and select **NVIDIA Control Panel**.

- Alternatively, you can open it through the **Start menu** by searching for "NVIDIA Control Panel".

Adjusting Settings:

- Go to **Manage 3D Settings** and adjust the following for better gaming performance:

  o **Power Management Mode**: Set it to **Prefer Maximum Performance**.

  o **Vertical Sync (V-Sync)**: Set this to **Off** if you want higher frame rates in fast-paced games.

  o **Texture Filtering**: Set it to **Performance** to reduce the GPU load.

Managing Frame Rates, Resolution, and Input Lag

Managing **frame rates**, **resolution**, and **input lag** is crucial for a smooth gaming experience. Here's how to optimize these settings.

Using G-Sync to Ensure Smooth Gameplay and Eliminate Screen Tearing

What G-Sync does:

- **G-Sync** synchronizes your **GPU's frame output** with your **monitor's refresh rate**, eliminating **screen tearing** and reducing **input lag** for smoother gameplay.

How to enable G-Sync:

- Open **NVIDIA Control Panel** (Right-click on the desktop).

- Go to **Display** → **Set up G-Sync**.
- Check **Enable G-Sync**, and select your monitor (make sure it supports G-Sync).
- Apply the settings.

How to Choose the Right Refresh Rate and Resolution for 4K or FHD Gaming

Choosing Resolution:

- **FHD (1920 x 1080)** is great for **smooth gameplay** at **high frame rates**, especially in **fast-paced games**.

- **4K (3840 x 2160)** provides **ultra-sharp visuals** but requires more GPU power to maintain high frame rates.

Choosing Refresh Rate:

- For **FHD gaming**, aim for **120Hz** or **165Hz** for **smooth and responsive gameplay**.

- For **4K gaming**, you might want to reduce the refresh rate to **60Hz** or **120Hz**, as **4K gaming** is demanding on the system.

Troubleshooting Frame Drops, Input Lag, and Performance Bottlenecks

Frame Drops:

- If you experience **frame drops**, try reducing **graphics settings** or switching to a **lower resolution**.

- Use **NVIDIA Control Panel** to turn off any unnecessary background processes.

Input Lag:

- **Input lag** can be reduced by enabling **G-Sync** or reducing **V-Sync** in the game settings.

Advanced Gaming Features: Streaming, Recording, and More

Razer Blade 16 with **NVIDIA RTX graphics** provides powerful features for **live streaming** and **recording gameplay**. Here's how to use them.

Using GeForce Experience and ShadowPlay to Stream Games

GeForce Experience:

- Download **GeForce Experience** from the **NVIDIA website**.

- Log in or create an **NVIDIA account**.

ShadowPlay for Streaming:

- Open **GeForce Experience**, go to the **Share** tab, and enable **ShadowPlay**.

- Click the **Start Streaming** button to start broadcasting your gameplay on **Twitch**, **YouTube**, or other platforms.

How to Record Gameplay:

- With **ShadowPlay**, click **Alt + Z** to bring up the **overlay**.

- Click **Record** to capture gameplay footage for sharing.

Setting Up NVIDIA Broadcast for Streaming with AI Features (Noise Removal, Auto Framing)

Download NVIDIA Broadcast:

- Download **NVIDIA Broadcast** from the **NVIDIA website**.

- Install and open the app.

Noise Removal:

- In **NVIDIA Broadcast**, go to **Audio** settings and enable **Noise Removal** to clean up your microphone audio.

Auto Framing:

- In **NVIDIA Broadcast**, go to **Webcam** settings and enable **Auto Framing**, which will automatically center and follow your face during a stream.

How to Record High-Quality Game Clips for Social Media or Content Creation

Using ShadowPlay for High-Quality Clips:

- Open **GeForce Experience** and go to the **Share** tab.

- Click on **Record** and select **Highlight** or **Manual Recording** to capture gameplay footage.

- Save clips directly to **social media** platforms or **video editors** for content creation.

By following these **step-by-step instructions**, you can **optimize your Razer Blade 16 for gaming**, configure your **NVIDIA RTX GPU settings**, manage **frame rates** and **resolution**, and even **stream and record gameplay** with **GeForce Experience** and **NVIDIA Broadcast**. With these settings, you'll be able to enjoy **high-quality gaming performance** on your laptop.

Chapter 5

Software for Creators: Content Creation on the Blade 16

The **Razer Blade 16** is an excellent tool for **creators**, offering powerful hardware and a high-quality display to support various content creation tasks. Whether you're into **video editing**, **graphic design**, or **audio production**, this guide will walk you through how to set up and use the right software to enhance your creative workflow.

Setting Up for Video Editing

Video editing requires the right tools and optimization to ensure smooth, fast, and efficient workflows. In this section, we'll walk through installing **Adobe Premiere Pro** and **DaVinci Resolve**, configuring **GPU acceleration**, and ensuring **color accuracy** in your **video editing projects**.

Installing and Optimizing Adobe Premiere Pro

Adobe Premiere Pro is one of the most powerful video editing tools available for professionals and beginners alike. Here's how to install and optimize it for video editing on the **Razer Blade 16**:

Step 1: Installing Adobe Premiere Pro

1. **Go to Adobe's website**: Open a web browser and go to **adobe.com**.

2. **Download Creative Cloud**: Once on the site, navigate to the **Creative Cloud** section and click on **Download**. This app will manage your installations of all Adobe software.

3. **Install Creative Cloud**: Run the downloaded installer to install **Creative Cloud**.

4. **Sign in or Create an Adobe Account**: Open the **Creative Cloud app** and sign in with your **Adobe account**. If you don't have one, click **Create an Account** and follow the prompts.

5. **Install Premiere Pro**: After logging in, go to the **Apps** section in **Creative Cloud**, find **Premiere Pro**, and click **Install**.

Step 2: Optimizing Adobe Premiere Pro for GPU Acceleration

Enable GPU Acceleration: Premiere Pro can leverage your **GPU** (Graphics Processing Unit) for faster rendering and smoother editing.

6. Open **Premiere Pro**.

7. Go to **File → Project Settings → General**.

8. In the **Renderer** section, select **Mercury Playback Engine GPU Acceleration (CUDA)** to use your **GPU** for rendering.

9. Click **OK** to apply the changes.

Tip for beginners: Enabling **GPU Acceleration** can dramatically reduce **rendering times** and **increase playback performance**.

Step 3: Customizing the Display for Color Accuracy in Video Editing

10. **Step 1**: Calibrate your **display** to ensure that the colors you see while editing are accurate. This is important when working on professional video projects where color grading is crucial.

11. **Step 2**: On your **Razer Blade 16**, go to **Settings** → **System** → **Display** and click on **Advanced Display Settings**.

12. **Step 3**: Scroll down to **Color Calibration** and click **Calibrate Display**.

13. **Step 4**: Follow the instructions in the **Display Color Calibration Wizard** to adjust **brightness**, **contrast**, and **color balance** for the most accurate display possible.

14. **Tip for beginners**: Use **Adobe RGB** or **sRGB** color profiles in Premiere Pro to keep your colors consistent.

Installing and Optimizing DaVinci Resolve

DaVinci Resolve is a **free** video editing software known for its powerful color grading and editing capabilities. Here's how to install and optimize it on your **Razer Blade 16**:

Step 1: Installing DaVinci Resolve

1. **Download DaVinci Resolve**: Go to the **Blackmagic Design website** (blackmagicdesign.com) and navigate to the **DaVinci Resolve** section.

2. **Choose the Version**: Select **Free Version** (unless you want to upgrade to the paid version) and click **Download**.

3. **Install DaVinci Resolve**: Once downloaded, open the installer and follow the on-screen instructions to complete the installation.

Step 2: Optimize GPU Acceleration in DaVinci Resolve

1. Open **DaVinci Resolve**.

2. Go to **Preferences** → **System** → **Memory and GPU**.

3. Under **GPU Processing Mode**, select **CUDA** (if you're using an NVIDIA GPU) or **OpenCL** (for AMD GPUs).

4. Restart **DaVinci Resolve** to apply the settings.

Photo and Graphic Design

For **graphic design** and **photo editing**, your **Razer Blade 16** is equipped with powerful software like **Photoshop**, **Lightroom**, and **Illustrator**. Here's how to install and set them up to get the most out of their features.

Setting Up Photoshop, Lightroom, Illustrator for Creative Professionals

Adobe Photoshop, **Lightroom**, and **Illustrator** are essential tools for **graphic design** and **photo editing**. Let's go through how to install and configure them for creative work.

Installing Photoshop and Lightroom:

- **Step 1: Install via Creative Cloud**

    o Open **Creative Cloud** and go to the **Apps** tab.

    o Find **Photoshop** and **Lightroom** and click **Install**.

- **Step 2: Launch the Applications**: Once the installation is complete, open **Photoshop** and **Lightroom**.

Installing Illustrator:

- **Step 1: Install via Creative Cloud**

    o Go to the **Creative Cloud** app and find **Illustrator** in the **Apps** tab.

    o Click **Install**.

- **Step 2: Launch Illustrator**: Once installed, open **Illustrator** and sign in with your **Adobe account**.

Working with High-Resolution Files and Managing Color Profiles

When working on **high-resolution images** or **graphic design projects**, color accuracy and file handling are crucial.

Managing Color Profiles:

- **Step 1**: Open **Photoshop** or **Illustrator** and navigate to **Edit → Color Settings**.

- **Step 2**: Set your **RGB Working Space** to **Adobe RGB** or **sRGB** (depending on your project).

- **Step 3**: This will ensure that colors are consistent and accurate across devices.

- **Tip for beginners**: Use **Photoshop's built-in proofing tools** to simulate how your colors will look on different displays or printers.

Working with High-Resolution Files:

- **Step 1**: For **large files** (e.g., 4K images), ensure that your laptop has **enough memory** allocated for these files. Open **Task Manager** and monitor your **RAM usage** to avoid overloading the system.

- **Step 2**: In **Photoshop**, try to keep layers minimal and use **smart objects** to avoid unnecessary performance hits when editing high-resolution files.

Optimizing the Blade 16 for 3D Rendering and Graphic Design Projects

For **3D rendering** and **complex graphic design**, it's essential to have **optimized GPU usage**:

Optimizing for 3D Rendering:

- **Step 1**: Open **Razer Synapse**.

- **Step 2**: Go to **Performance** → **GPU Settings** and set your GPU to **Maximum Performance**.

- **Step 3**: In **Blender, Maya**, or any 3D software, enable **GPU Rendering** for faster performance.

Audio Production and Recording

For **audio production** and **recording, Razer Blade 16** offers all the necessary tools to get professional results. Let's walk through how to install **Audacity, Adobe Audition**, and set up **audio input/output** for **high-quality sound**.

Using Audacity, Adobe Audition, and Other Audio Editing Software

Installing Audacity:

- **Step 1**: Go to the **Audacity website** (audacityteam.org) and download the latest version.

- **Step 2**: Run the installer and follow the on-screen instructions.

- **Step 3**: Once installed, launch **Audacity** and set up your audio devices.

Installing Adobe Audition:

- **Step 1**: Open **Creative Cloud** and find **Audition** in the **Apps** tab.

- **Step 2**: Click **Install**, and once the installation is complete, open **Audition**.

- **Step 3**: Configure the audio settings by selecting your **microphone** and **headphones** in the **Preferences** menu.

Managing Audio Inputs and Outputs for High-Quality Recording

To ensure **clean and professional-quality recordings**, it's essential to properly configure your **audio inputs and outputs**.

Step 1: Set Up Audio Input (Microphone):

1. Open **Audacity** or **Adobe Audition**.

2. Navigate to **Preferences** → **Devices** and select your **microphone** or **audio interface** as the input device.

Step 2: Check the **input gain** to ensure the microphone is at an appropriate level without clipping.

Step 3: Set Up Audio Output (Headphones or Speakers):

1. In **Audacity** or **Audition**, navigate to **Preferences** → **Devices** and set your

headphones or **external speakers** as the output device.

Configuring External Audio Equipment for Studio-Grade Sound

For **high-quality sound, studio-grade microphones** and **audio interfaces** are essential. Here's how to connect and optimize external equipment:

Step 1: Connect External Audio Gear:

1. Plug in your **microphone** or **audio interface** into the **USB or XLR ports** on the **Razer Blade 16**.
2. **Step 2**: Open **Audacity** or **Adobe Audition**, and in the **Preferences** menu, select your **audio interface** as the input device.

Step 3: Set Gain Levels:

1. Adjust the **gain** on your **audio interface** to ensure your microphone's volume is optimal. Avoid turning the gain too high, as this can cause distortion.

By following these **step-by-step instructions**, you're ready to make the most of your **Razer Blade 16** for **content creation**. Whether you're editing **videos** in **Adobe Premiere Pro**, designing **graphics** in **Photoshop** and **Illustrator**, or producing **high-quality audio**, your laptop is now optimized for creative work.

Chapter 6

Business Productivity: Maximizing Efficiency

In this section, we break down **essential business software** and provide a detailed **setup guide** for each, covering the following tools: **Microsoft Office 365, Google Workspace, QuickBooks, Xero, FreshBooks, HubSpot, Salesforce**, and **security tools**.

Essential Business Software Setup

These essential tools for collaboration, communication, and project management will enhance your business productivity.

Microsoft Office 365 for Word, Excel, PowerPoint, Outlook

Microsoft Office 365 includes the powerful apps: **Word, Excel, PowerPoint**, and **Outlook**, which are commonly used for business tasks like document creation, data analysis, presentations, and managing emails.

Step 1: Sign up for Microsoft 365

1. Go to **Microsoft 365 Website**.

2. Select **Business** or **Personal** plans, based on your needs.

3. Click **Buy Now** or **Start Free Trial** if available.

4. **Create a Microsoft Account** or log into an existing one.

Step 2: Install Office Apps

1. After signing in, navigate to **"Install Office"**.

2. Download the **installer** for Office 365.

3. Run the installer, which will automatically download and install all core apps (Word, Excel, PowerPoint, Outlook).

4. Once the installation is complete, open any Office application, and sign in with your Microsoft account to activate it.

Step 3: Use Office 365 Applications

1. **Word**: Start creating professional documents. You can use templates or create from scratch. **Save files** on OneDrive for cloud access.

2. **Excel**: Create spreadsheets for budgeting, analysis, and reports. Use formulas and templates.

3. **PowerPoint**: Build presentations for meetings, proposals, and reports. Use slide transitions and animations.

4. **Outlook**: Set up and manage your email. Organize calendars, schedule meetings, and use task lists to stay organized.

Google Workspace for Cloud-Based Collaboration (Docs, Sheets, Drive)

Google Workspace provides tools like **Docs, Sheets, Drive**, and **Gmail**, making it easier to work collaboratively and store files in the cloud.

Step 1: Sign up for Google Workspace

1. Go to **Google Workspace** and click on **Get Started**.

2. Choose a **business plan** and enter **business information**.

3. Sign in with your **Google account** or create a new one.

Step 2: Set Up Google Apps

1. **Google Docs**: Create documents like Word, with the ability to collaborate in real time. **Share** the document by adding collaborators' email addresses.

2. **Google Sheets**: Use for spreadsheets, similar to Excel. Create and edit data, and track information using formulas.

3. **Google Drive**: Store all your documents, spreadsheets, presentations, etc. on the cloud. You can share files and organize them into folders.

4. **Google Calendar**: Set meetings, appointments, and reminders, and share them with your team.

Step 3: Collaborate in Real-Time

- Work simultaneously with your team on **Docs** and **Sheets**. All changes are updated in real-time.

Finance and Accounting Tools for Business Owners

Effective financial management is essential for business success. Here's how to set up and use popular finance tools like **QuickBooks, Xero**, and **FreshBooks**.

QuickBooks for Business Finances

QuickBooks is one of the most popular accounting tools that can help you manage your business finances, track expenses, create invoices, and handle payroll.

Step 1: Sign Up for QuickBooks

1. Go to **QuickBooks Website**.

2. Choose a **plan** (QuickBooks Self-Employed, QuickBooks Online Simple Start, etc.) depending on your business needs.

3. Click **Start Free Trial** or **Buy Now**.

4. Sign up with your **email address** and **create an account**.

Step 2: Set Up Your Company Profile

1. After signing in, you will be prompted to enter your **business information** (name, type, address).

2. Select the **accounting method** (cash or accrual) and **tax settings**.

3. Link your **bank accounts** and **credit cards** to automatically import and categorize transactions.

Step 3: Manage Finances

1. **Track Expenses**: Add transactions and categorize them (e.g., office supplies, payroll).

2. **Create Invoices**: Set up **professional invoices** with your business logo and send them directly from QuickBooks.

3. **Generate Reports**: Use **reports** like profit & loss statements, balance sheets, and tax reports for better financial insights.

Xero for Cloud Accounting

Xero is another powerful tool that helps manage your **finances**, **invoices**, **expenses**, and **payroll** from anywhere.

Step 1: Sign Up for Xero

1. Visit **Xero Website**.

2. Select a **plan** (Starter, Standard, or Premium) based on your needs.

3. Sign up using your **email address** and create your **Xero account**.

Step 2: Set Up Xero for Your Business

1. **Enter Your Business Details**: Fill out your **business name**, **address**, and **tax information**.

2. **Connect Your Bank Accounts**: Link your bank accounts and credit cards to automatically import transactions.

3. **Set Up Payroll**: If your business has employees, you can set up **payroll** to pay them directly through Xero.

Step 3: Manage Finances

1. **Track Transactions**: Record **sales** and **expenses**, and use the **bank reconciliation feature** to match them to your bank statements.

2. **Create Invoices and Quotes**: Send **invoices** and **quotes** directly from Xero. Customize them with your company branding.

FreshBooks for Invoicing and Accounting

FreshBooks simplifies **invoicing, expense tracking**, and **project management** for small businesses and freelancers.

Step 1: Sign Up for FreshBooks

1. Visit **FreshBooks Website**.

2. Choose your plan (e.g., Lite, Plus, Premium) and create your **FreshBooks account**.

Step 2: Set Up Your FreshBooks Account

1. **Enter Business Details**: Add your **business name, address**, and **tax information**.

2. **Connect Bank Accounts**: Link your **bank accounts** to track expenses and payments automatically.

Step 3: Create Invoices

1. **Create Professional Invoices**: Design and send **invoices** with your company logo. **Track payment statuses** and set **payment reminders** for overdue invoices.

Step 4: Expense Tracking

1. **Track Expenses**: Add expenses like receipts and categorize them for easy tracking and tax deductions.

CRM and Sales Management

CRM tools are designed to help businesses manage **customer relationships**, **track sales**, and **automate tasks**. Let's look at setting up **HubSpot** and **Salesforce**.

HubSpot for CRM and Lead Management

HubSpot is a free and easy-to-use CRM tool that helps you manage customer relationships, track leads, and automate sales workflows.

Step 1: Sign Up for HubSpot

1. Visit **HubSpot Website**.

2. Create a free **HubSpot account** or sign up for a paid version for advanced features.

Step 2: Set Up Your HubSpot Account

1. Once signed up, you can start by creating your **contact database**. Add **customer information**, **deal stages**, and **sales pipelines**.

Step 3: Manage Leads and Sales

1. **Track Leads**: Capture leads via forms on your website and manage them in the CRM.

2. **Automate Tasks**: Set up **automated emails** and **follow-up reminders** to nurture leads.

Salesforce for Sales Management and Customer Tracking

Salesforce is a powerful CRM and sales tool, offering robust customization options to manage leads, sales, and customer relationships.

Step 1: Sign Up for Salesforce

1. Visit **Salesforce Website**.

2. Choose a plan (Salesforce Essentials or other options depending on business needs) and sign up.

Step 2: Set Up Salesforce

1. After logging in, set up your **custom sales pipeline**, including stages like **Lead**, **Opportunity**, and **Closed**.

2. **Add Contacts**: Import your customer list and create custom fields to track relevant customer data.

Step 3: Manage Leads and Sales

1. **Track Sales**: View and manage **leads, opportunities**, and **deals** in Salesforce's intuitive interface.

2. **Automate Follow-ups**: Use **Salesforce's workflow automation** to send follow-up emails and reminders based on customer behavior.

Security and Privacy in Business

Security software is crucial to protect your business data from threats. Here's how to set up **antivirus software**, use **VPNs**, and manage **passwords**.

Installing Antivirus Software

Antivirus software protects your computer from viruses, malware, and cyber-attacks.

Step 1: Choose an Antivirus Provider

1. Popular options include **Norton, McAfee, Bitdefender**.

2. Visit the provider's website and purchase a plan.

Step 2: Install Antivirus Software

1. After purchasing, download the installer from the provider's website.

2. Follow the installation prompts and set up the software.

Step 3: Run Initial Scan

1. Once installed, run a **full system scan** to detect any potential threats. Set up **real-time protection**

to continuously monitor your system for security threats.

Using VPNs for Secure Browsing

A **VPN** (Virtual Private Network) encrypts your internet connection and ensures secure browsing, especially when working on **public Wi-Fi**.

Step 1: Choose a VPN Provider

1. Options include **NordVPN**, **ExpressVPN**, **CyberGhost**.

2. Download the provider's software and sign up for a plan.

Step 2: Install VPN Software

1. Follow the installation instructions on the website.

2. **Step 3: Connect to a Secure Server**

   o Open the VPN app, select a server, and click **Connect** to secure your internet connection.

Password Management with LastPass, 1Password

Using a **password manager** ensures your passwords are stored securely and allows easy access to your business logins.

Step 1: Choose a Password Manager

1. Popular options include **LastPass, 1Password**, or **Dashlane**.

Step 2: Install the Password Manager

1. Download the **LastPass** or **1Password** browser extension or desktop app.

2. Sign up for an account and create a **master password**.

Step 3: Add Passwords to the Vault

1. Add all your business-related accounts (email, CRM, financial tools) to the password vault.

2. Enable **two-factor authentication (2FA)** for extra security.

With the tools and software outlined in this chapter, your **business productivity** will be optimized across various areas: **collaboration, finance management, sales tracking**, and **security**. Setting up the right tools will help streamline your business processes, improve efficiency, and ensure that your business operations are secure.

Chapter 7

Advanced Software Development Tools

This chapter provides comprehensive, **beginner-friendly** instructions to help you set up a robust development environment and manage cloud applications. We'll guide you through installing essential tools such as **IDEs, Git, Docker, Kubernetes**, and managing your **cloud infrastructure** and **network configurations**.

Setting Up for Software Development

Before diving into software development, you need the right tools. This section will walk you through installing **IDEs (Integrated Development Environments)** such as **VSCode, JetBrains**, and **Eclipse**. Additionally, we'll set up **Git** for version control.

Installing IDEs (VSCode, JetBrains Suite, Eclipse) for Coding

An **IDE** is a software application that provides comprehensive facilities for software development, such as coding, debugging, and testing. Below are steps to install **VSCode, JetBrains**, and **Eclipse**.

Step 1: Installing VSCode

1. Go to the **VSCode website**: https://code.visualstudio.com.

2. Download the **installer** for your operating system (Windows, macOS, or Linux).

3. Run the installer and follow the **setup wizard** to install **VSCode**.

4. Once installed, open **VSCode**, and you will see a basic editor ready to use.

5. Install necessary **extensions** like Python, JavaScript, or C# based on the languages you will be using. You can find these extensions in the **Extensions Marketplace** within VSCode.

Step 2: Installing JetBrains Suite

1. Visit the **JetBrains website**: https://www.jetbrains.com.

2. Choose the appropriate JetBrains tool for your needs (e.g., **IntelliJ IDEA, PyCharm, WebStorm**).

3. Download and install your selected IDE (you may be able to use a **free trial** or use the **Community edition**).

4. Launch the IDE, and you'll be prompted to configure it based on your preferences, such as setting up programming languages and enabling plugins.

Step 3: Installing Eclipse

1. Go to the **Eclipse download page**: https://www.eclipse.org/downloads.

2. Download the **Eclipse IDE for Java Developers** (or another version, depending on your needs).

3. Install Eclipse by running the installer. Follow the on-screen instructions to complete the setup.

4. Once installed, launch **Eclipse**, and you can start coding by creating new **Java projects** or other types of development environments.

Managing Projects with Git and GitHub: Best Practices for Version Control

Git is a **version control system** that helps you manage and track changes to your codebase. **GitHub** is a platform that hosts Git repositories and allows for collaboration. Let's walk through the process of setting up **Git** and using **GitHub**.

Step 1: Installing Git

1. Go to the **Git website**: https://git-scm.com.

2. Download the latest version of **Git** for your operating system (Windows, macOS, or Linux).

3. Run the installer and follow the default installation steps.

Step 2: Setting Up Git

1. Open your **Terminal (macOS/Linux)** or **Git Bash (Windows)**.

2. Configure your Git settings by entering the following commands:

- o git config --global user.name "Your Name"

- o git config --global user.email "your.email@example.com"

3. Verify the configuration with the command: git config --list.

Step 3: Using GitHub for Collaboration

1. Go to **GitHub** and create a free account.

2. Create a **new repository** by clicking the **New** button in your dashboard.

3. Clone the repository to your local machine:

   - o Use the command git clone <repository-url>.

4. Make changes to your code and commit them:

   - o Stage changes: git add .

   - o Commit changes: git commit -m "Your commit message"

   - o Push changes to GitHub: git push origin main

5. You can also create **branches** and open **pull requests** to collaborate with others.

Using Docker and Kubernetes for Cloud Development

Docker and **Kubernetes** are essential tools for managing and deploying cloud-based applications. Docker helps you create **containers**, while Kubernetes manages and orchestrates those containers.

Installing Docker and Setting Up Containers for Development Environments

Docker allows you to package applications into containers, ensuring that your software runs the same on any system.

Step 1: Installing Docker

1. Go to the **Docker website**: https://www.docker.com.

2. Download the Docker Desktop application for your operating system (Windows/macOS).

3. Run the installer and follow the instructions to install **Docker Desktop**.

4. Once installed, open **Docker Desktop**. You should see a Docker icon in your system tray indicating that Docker is running.

Step 2: Creating a Docker Container

1. Open your **Terminal (macOS/Linux)** or **Docker Command Line Interface**.

2. Use the command docker run hello-world to verify that Docker is running properly.

3. To create your own container, use the following basic command:

- o docker run -d -p 80:80 --name my-container nginx

- o This command will create a container running **Nginx** (a web server) and map it to port **80** on your local machine.

4. To see a list of all running containers, use:

- o docker ps

5. To stop a container, use:

- o docker stop my-container

Managing Cloud Resources with Kubernetes

Kubernetes is a powerful platform used to orchestrate the deployment, scaling, and management of Docker containers.

Step 1: Installing Kubernetes

1. Install **Minikube**, a tool that sets up a local Kubernetes cluster for development:

- o Follow the **Minikube installation guide**: https://minikube.sigs.k8s.io/docs/.

2. Install **kubectl**, the command-line tool for interacting with Kubernetes clusters:

- o Install using this command: brew install kubectl (for macOS) or follow the installation guide for your OS.

Step 2: Setting Up Kubernetes Cluster with Minikube

1. Start your Kubernetes cluster with the command:

   o minikube start

2. Verify that the cluster is running by typing:

   o kubectl cluster-info

3. Deploy a containerized application:

   o Use the following command to create a **deployment** in Kubernetes:

      ▪ kubectl create deployment my-app --image=nginx

4. Expose the application to your local system:

   o kubectl expose deployment my-app --type=NodePort --port=80

5. You can then access your deployed application at the NodePort.

Cloud Platforms for Development

Cloud platforms like **AWS**, **Azure**, and **GCP** provide the infrastructure for deploying and managing applications in the cloud. This section will walk you through setting up cloud environments for development.

Setting Up AWS, Azure, and GCP for Application Hosting and Development

Step 1: Setting Up AWS

1. Go to **AWS website** and create an **AWS account**.

2. After logging in, navigate to **AWS Management Console**.

3. To create a virtual server (EC2 instance), click on **EC2** and then **Launch Instance**.

4. Choose an **AMI (Amazon Machine Image)**, such as **Amazon Linux 2** or **Ubuntu**.

5. Set up your **instance type** (e.g., t2. micro for basic usage).

6. Configure security settings, including **key pair** for SSH access.

7. Once the instance is running, you can SSH into it using the provided **public IP address**.

Step 2: Setting Up Azure

1. Visit **Azure website** and sign up for an account.

2. Go to the **Azure portal** and select **Create a resource**.

3. Choose a **virtual machine** (VM) image like **Ubuntu** or **Windows Server**.

4. Set up the **VM size** and **region**.

5. Configure networking and security settings, then click **Create**.

6. After the VM is created, connect to it using **SSH** or **Remote Desktop**.

Step 3: Setting Up GCP

1. Visit **GCP website** and sign up for an account.

2. Navigate to **Google Cloud Console** and create a **new project**.

3. Go to **Compute Engine**, then click **Create Instance**.

4. Select the **OS** and **machine type** (e.g., f1-micro for lightweight workloads).

5. Configure firewall and networking, then click **Create**.

6. Once the instance is running, connect to it using **SSH** from the GCP console.

Deploying and Managing Applications on Cloud Servers

1. **AWS**: Use **Elastic Beanstalk** for easy deployment and management of applications.

2. **Azure**: Use **Azure App Services** to deploy web applications easily.

3. **GCP**: Use **Google Kubernetes Engine (GKE)** to manage containerized applications.

Network Configuration and IT Management

Managing your IT networks and automating administrative tasks can save time and effort. Below are instructions for managing network tasks using **PowerShell** (for Windows) and **Bash scripts** (for Linux/macOS).

Using Windows PowerShell and Bash for Network Administration

Step 1: PowerShell for Network Management (Windows)

1. Open **PowerShell** as **Administrator** by right-clicking the Start button and selecting **Windows PowerShell (Admin)**.

2. To check network configuration:

   o Run Get-NetIPAddress to see IP address configurations.

3. To configure network settings:

   o Use Set-NetIPAddress to set a new IP address.

   o For example, to set a static IP: Set-NetIPAddress -InterfaceAlias "Ethernet" -IPAddress 192.168.1.100 -PrefixLength 24 -DefaultGateway 192.168.1.1.

Step 2: Bash Scripts for Network Management (Linux/macOS)

1. Open **Terminal** on **Linux** or **macOS**.

2. To view IP configurations:

   o Run ifconfig (or ip a on newer systems).

3. To set a static IP address:

   o Edit the /etc/network/interfaces or use the nmcli command (for **NetworkManager**).

Automating Server Tasks with Task Schedulers and Bash Scripts

1. **Windows Task Scheduler**: Use it to automate tasks like backups or system scans.

   o Open **Task Scheduler**, create a **new task**, and set it to run at specific times or events.

2. **Automating with Bash**:

   o Create a script (e.g., backup.sh) and add commands to automate tasks.

   o Use cron jobs (Linux/macOS) to schedule the script to run periodically.

   o For example, to schedule a backup every day at midnight, use:

   `bash`

   crontab -e

   0 0 * * * /path/to/backup.sh

This chapter covered essential tools for **software development, cloud application management**, and **IT network configuration**. By following these steps, you'll be equipped to set up a development environment, manage cloud resources, and automate tasks for a smooth and efficient workflow.

These tools—**VSCode, Git, Docker, Kubernetes**, and cloud platforms—will help you build, deploy, and manage applications efficiently, and the **PowerShell** and

Bash scripting will automate and streamline network and server management tasks.

Chapter 8

Cloud Integration and Mobile Devices

This chapter will help you integrate **cloud-based services** and **mobile devices** with your **Razer Blade 16** for a seamless, efficient, and productive experience. We will cover **cloud gaming setup**, **cloud storage solutions**, and how to **sync mobile devices** with your Blade 16 for easier file management and access.

Cloud Gaming Setup

Cloud gaming allows you to play high-end games without needing powerful local hardware. This section will walk you through setting up **GeForce NOW** and **Xbox Cloud Gaming** for seamless cloud-based gaming on your **Razer Blade 16**.

Using GeForce NOW and Xbox Cloud Gaming for Cloud-based Gaming

GeForce NOW and **Xbox Cloud Gaming** (formerly known as **xCloud**) are popular cloud gaming platforms that allow you to stream games from the cloud to your device, minimizing the need for high-powered hardware.

Step 1: Setting Up GeForce NOW for Cloud Gaming

1. **Sign Up for GeForce NOW**:

- o Visit the **GeForce NOW website**: https://www.nvidia.com/en-us/geforce-now.

- o Click **Join Now** and create a **NVIDIA account** if you don't already have one.

- o Choose the appropriate **subscription plan** (Free, Priority, or RTX 3080 for the highest performance).

2. **Install the GeForce NOW App**:

- o After signing up, download and install the **GeForce NOW app** for Windows from the website.

- o **Run the installer** and follow the setup instructions to install it.

3. **Log in and Start Gaming**:

- o Open **GeForce NOW**, sign in with your NVIDIA account, and link your **Steam** or **Epic Games** accounts.

- o Browse through the list of supported games (you can also add games from your library) and **start playing** without needing to install them on your local machine.

- o Ensure your internet speed meets the required **minimum bandwidth** (usually 15-25 Mbps for optimal performance).

4. **Tip for beginners**: A **wired Ethernet connection** or a **strong Wi-Fi connection**

(preferably 5GHz) will enhance streaming quality and minimize lag.

Step 2: Setting Up Xbox Cloud Gaming (xCloud)

1. **Sign Up for Xbox Cloud Gaming**:

   o Go to **Xbox Cloud Gaming**: https://www.xbox.com/en-US/play.

   o **Sign in with your Microsoft account** or create a new one.

   o **Subscribe to Xbox Game Pass Ultimate**, which gives you access to **Xbox Cloud Gaming**.

2. **Using Xbox Cloud Gaming on Blade 16**:

   o Open a web browser (e.g., Chrome, Edge) on your **Blade 16** and visit the **Xbox Cloud Gaming** website.

   o Log in with your **Microsoft account** and browse the available games.

   o **Click Play** to launch a game directly in your browser and start gaming.

3. **Tip for beginners**: Xbox Cloud Gaming runs through a browser, so make sure to have the **latest browser version** installed for smooth performance.

Cloud Storage for Business and Creative Work

Cloud storage is crucial for storing, syncing, and collaborating on files across devices. In this section, we'll cover how to **sync files** between **Google Drive**, **OneDrive**, and **Dropbox**, and best practices for collaborative cloud workspaces.

Syncing Files Across Devices with Google Drive, OneDrive, and Dropbox

Step 1: Setting Up Google Drive

1. **Install Google Drive**:

    o   Go to the **Google Drive website**: https://www.google.com/drive/.

    o   Click on **Download** to get **Google Drive for Desktop**.

    o   **Install the app** and sign in with your **Google account**.

2. **Sync Files with Google Drive**:

    o   Once installed, Google Drive will create a **Drive folder** on your computer.

    o   **Drag and drop** files into this folder to automatically sync them with the cloud.

    o   You can access your files from any device by visiting **Google Drive** via your browser or the mobile app.

3. **Collaborative Features**:

- o Share files and folders with team members, giving them **edit** or **view-only** permissions.

Step 2: Setting Up OneDrive

1. **Install OneDrive**:

   - o Visit **OneDrive Website**.

   - o Download the **OneDrive** app for **Windows** or **macOS**.

   - o Sign in with your **Microsoft account**.

2. **Sync Files with OneDrive**:

   - o Once installed, OneDrive will create a **OneDrive folder** on your computer.

   - o **Drag and drop** files to the OneDrive folder, and they will sync to the cloud.

3. **Collaborative Features**:

   - o Use **Microsoft 365 apps** (Word, Excel, PowerPoint) to collaborate in real-time on shared documents.

Step 3: Setting Up Dropbox

1. **Install Dropbox**:

   - o Go to the **Dropbox website** and sign up for an account.

   - o Download and install the **Dropbox app** on your **Blade 16**.

2. **Sync Files with Dropbox**:

- o Once installed, Dropbox creates a **Dropbox folder** where you can drop files for syncing.

- o Dropbox syncs your files automatically to the cloud, making them available across devices.

3. **Collaborative Features**:

- o Share files and folders by right-clicking in the **Dropbox folder**, selecting **Share**, and sending the link to collaborators.

Best Practices for Collaborative Cloud Workspaces

1. **Google Docs** and **Office 365** are great for real-time collaboration. Share documents with team members, leave comments, and track changes to keep everyone on the same page.

2. **Use cloud storage efficiently**:

- o Keep **organized folders** for easy access.

- o Use file names and tags to easily find documents.

- o Enable **automatic backups** to ensure nothing is lost.

Mobile Device Sync and Integration

Syncing your **Razer Blade 16** with mobile devices can increase productivity by allowing easy access to files, apps, and other data between devices. This section will walk you through syncing files and apps between your **Blade 16** and your mobile device.

How to Sync Files and Apps Between the Blade 16 and Mobile Devices

Step 1: Syncing Files with Google Drive, OneDrive, and Dropbox on Mobile Devices

1. **Google Drive**:

    o   Install the **Google Drive app** on your mobile device from the **Google Play Store** (Android) or **App Store** (iOS).

    o   Sign in with the same **Google account** you use on your **Blade 16**.

    o   Any files uploaded to **Google Drive** on your PC will sync to the mobile app and vice versa.

2. **OneDrive**:

    o   Install the **OneDrive app** on your mobile device.

    o   Sign in with the same **Microsoft account**.

    o   Files and folders in **OneDrive** will automatically sync between devices.

3. **Dropbox**:

    o   Install the **Dropbox app** on your mobile device.

o   Sign in with your **Dropbox account** to sync files between your Blade 16 and mobile devices.

Step 2: Syncing Apps Between Devices

1. **Syncing Calendar and Contacts**:

    o   For Google accounts, use **Google Calendar** and **Google Contacts** on your phone for seamless syncing.

    o   For Microsoft accounts, use **Outlook** and **Microsoft Calendar** to sync across your devices.

2. **Syncing Notes and Tasks**:

    o   Use apps like **Google Keep, Microsoft OneNote**, or **Evernote** to sync notes and tasks across devices. These apps have mobile apps that sync seamlessly with your **Blade 16**.

Managing Cloud Backups and Data Transfer Between Devices

1. **Backup your data**:

    o   Use **Google Photos** or **OneDrive** to back up photos and videos automatically from your mobile device to the cloud.

    o   Enable **automatic backups** on apps like **WhatsApp** or **iCloud** to ensure your important data is always secure.

2. **Transferring Data**:

103

o   **Android to Blade 16**: Use **Google Drive** or **USB cable** to transfer data from your Android device to the **Razer Blade 16**.

o   **iPhone to Blade 16**: Use **iCloud** for syncing or transfer data via **USB cable** using **iTunes** or **Finder**.

In this chapter, we've walked you through setting up **cloud gaming** with **GeForce NOW** and **Xbox Cloud Gaming**, syncing your **cloud storage** across devices, and connecting your **Razer Blade 16** with your mobile devices for a smooth and efficient workflow. By following these steps, you'll be able to enjoy seamless **cloud gaming**, keep your files in sync across all your devices, and easily integrate your Blade 16 with your phone or tablet—turning your laptop into the ultimate hub for both work and play.

Chapter 9

Tips, Tricks, and Advanced Customizations

In this chapter, we dive into **AI** and **automation**. These tools can significantly improve your productivity by reducing repetitive tasks, optimizing workflows, and even helping in creative tasks. Let's go step-by-step on how to **automate processes** using **AI-powered tools**.

AI and Automation

Leveraging AI for Optimizing Performance in Gaming and Creative Tasks

AI can be used in many areas to **optimize performance** and **improve efficiency**. Let's explore how you can use AI in **gaming** and **creative tasks**.

AI in Gaming: NVIDIA DLSS (Deep Learning Super Sampling)

AI in gaming can significantly improve the quality and performance of games. **NVIDIA's DLSS (Deep Learning Super Sampling)** is a prime example of how AI enhances gaming experience by improving performance without sacrificing visual quality.

How to Enable AI for Gaming Performance (DLSS):

1. **Ensure You Have a Compatible GPU:**

- o **DLSS** requires an **NVIDIA RTX graphics card**. If your Razer Blade 16 is equipped with one, you're set to take advantage of DLSS.

2. **Update Your Graphics Drivers**:

   - o **Download the latest NVIDIA drivers** from the NVIDIA website.

   - o Alternatively, use **GeForce Experience** to automatically download and install the latest drivers.

3. **Enable DLSS in Supported Games**:

   - o Open your game and go to **Graphics Settings**.

   - o Look for the **DLSS** option. It may be listed under **Graphics** or **Performance** settings, depending on the game.

   - o Select **DLSS** and choose a performance setting: **Quality**, **Balanced**, or **Performance** (for maximum performance).

4. **Benefits**:

   - o **DLSS** uses AI to upscale images, improving frame rates while maintaining high visual fidelity. This reduces the load on your GPU, resulting in better **gaming performance**.

AI in Creative Work: Adobe Photoshop's AI Features

Creative software like **Adobe Photoshop** uses AI to simplify editing tasks and help you achieve better results in less time.

Using Photoshop's AI Features:

1. **Adobe Sensei AI**:

    o **Adobe Sensei** powers many AI tools in Photoshop. Features like **Content-Aware Fill** or **Select Subject** are AI-driven, allowing for faster and more accurate editing.

2. **How to Use AI Features in Photoshop**:

    o Open **Photoshop** and select **Select Subject** under **Select** in the menu. Photoshop automatically detects the main subject in your image using AI, saving you time on manual selections.

    o **Content-Aware Fill**: If you want to remove an object, use the **Lasso Tool** to select the object, then go to **Edit** → **Fill** → **Content-Aware**. The AI will intelligently fill in the area.

3. **Benefits**:

    o Using AI in **Photoshop** improves your creative workflow, making tasks like object removal or background changes much easier and faster.

Automating Repetitive Tasks with Tools Like Zapier and IFTTT

Both **Zapier** and **IFTTT (If This Then That)** are tools designed to automate repetitive tasks across different apps, so you don't have to do the manual work. These platforms use **"triggers"** and **"actions"** to automate processes, making your work much more efficient.

Setting Up Automation with Zapier

Zapier is a tool that connects your favorite apps and automates tasks between them. Here's how to use it:

Step 1: Sign Up for Zapier

1. Go to Zapier's website and sign up for an account.

2. Choose your plan: there's a **free plan** and various **paid plans** depending on the level of automation you need.

Step 2: Creating Your First Zap (Automation)

1. Once logged in, click on **"Make a Zap"**. This will allow you to create your first automated task.

2. **Choose a Trigger**:

   o Select the **app** that will start your workflow (e.g., **Gmail**, **Google Drive**, or **Slack**).

   o For example, choose **Gmail** and set the trigger as **"New Email"**.

3. **Choose an Action**:

o   Select the **action** app where you want to send the data. For example, choose **Google Drive** and set the action as **"Save Attachment"**.

o   With this setup, every time you get a new email in Gmail, Zapier will automatically save any attachment to your **Google Drive**.

Step 3: Test and Activate Your Zap

1. After setting up the **trigger** and **action**, Zapier will ask you to test the automation to ensure everything works as expected.

2. If the test is successful, click **Turn On** to start your automation. Now, every time the trigger happens, your task will be performed automatically without any manual effort.

Example Use Cases:

*   **Save Email Attachments**: Automatically save email attachments to **Google Drive**.

*   **Create Calendar Events from Emails**: Automatically add events to **Google Calendar** when you receive emails with certain keywords.

*   **Post Social Media Updates**: Automatically post updates to **Twitter**, **Facebook**, or **LinkedIn** when you upload a new blog post.

Setting Up Automation with IFTTT (If This Then That)

IFTTT is another automation tool that connects apps and devices to create automated workflows.

Step 1: Sign Up for IFTTT

1. Visit the **IFTTT website** and sign up for a free account.

Step 2: Creating an Applet

1. Once signed in, click on **Create** to start a new **Applet** (automation).

2. Select the **"This"** service (the trigger) and choose an app like **Gmail**, **Google Sheets**, or **Weather**.

   o For example, choose **Gmail** as the trigger and select **"New Email in Inbox"**.

3. Choose the **"That"** service (the action), which is the app that will perform a task after the trigger occurs.

   o For example, choose **Google Sheets** and set the action to **"Add a row to a spreadsheet"**.

4. **Activate the Applet**:

   o After setting up the trigger and action, click **Finish** to activate your Applet. Now, when a new email arrives, IFTTT will automatically add the email's details into a **Google Sheets** document.

Example Use Cases:

- **Save Emails to Google Sheets**: Automatically log your emails into a **Google Sheets** document.

- **Control Smart Devices**: Automatically turn on your **smart lights** when the sun sets.

- **Weather Alerts**: Get an automatic text message or email every morning about the day's weather.

Using AI-Powered Apps for Improved Productivity (e.g., Grammarly, Jasper AI)

AI-powered apps can help improve your productivity by automating tasks and providing insights for optimization. Let's look at some apps that can boost productivity.

Grammarly: AI-Powered Writing Assistant

Grammarly helps improve your writing by providing suggestions for grammar, spelling, punctuation, and style.

How to Use Grammarly:

1. **Sign Up**: Go to **Grammarly** and sign up for an account.

2. **Install the Browser Extension**: Grammarly offers browser extensions for **Chrome**, **Firefox**, and **Edge**. Install it from the **Grammarly website**.

3. **Use Grammarly in Docs**:

- o When writing an email or document, Grammarly will automatically check your writing for errors in **real-time**.

- o It will underline errors and provide suggestions for correction.

4. **Upgrade to Premium for Advanced Features**:

- o For more advanced suggestions, such as **tone detection** or **clarity improvements**, you can subscribe to Grammarly's **Premium** version.

Benefits:

- Automatically improves writing by suggesting corrections for grammar, style, and clarity.

- Helps you sound more professional by catching awkward phrasing and poor punctuation.

Jasper AI: AI-Powered Content Creation

Jasper AI is a powerful content creation tool that uses AI to help generate articles, blog posts, social media content, and more.

How to Use Jasper AI:

1. **Sign Up**: Go to **Jasper** and create an account.

2. **Choose a Template**: Select the type of content you want to create, such as **blog posts**, **social media updates**, or **product descriptions**.

3. **Provide Input**: Jasper will ask for a **brief** about the topic, and you can adjust the tone, keywords, and length of the content you want to generate.

4. **Let Jasper Write for You**: After you input your brief, Jasper will automatically generate the content. You can tweak it as needed.

Benefits:

- Saves time by automating the content creation process.

- Provides AI-generated writing ideas and drafts for blog posts, social media, and more.

In this chapter, we've explored how to **automate tasks using AI**, optimize your **gaming experience** with **DLSS**, enhance your **creative workflow** with **Adobe Sensei**, and automate **repetitive tasks** using tools like **Zapier** and **IFTTT**. Additionally, we've covered how to use AI-powered apps like **Grammarly** and **Jasper AI** to enhance your **writing** and **content creation**.

By automating these processes, you can improve **productivity**, reduce manual effort, and get more done in less time, all while using the power of AI to enhance your overall workflow.

Chapter 10

Troubleshooting and Maintenance

In this chapter, we will cover everything you need to know about **troubleshooting common issues**, keeping your system in good health, ensuring your software and drivers are up-to-date, and providing advanced troubleshooting techniques. Following these steps will help you maintain the **optimal performance** of your **Razer Blade 16**.

Diagnosing and Fixing Common Issues

Even the best laptops can run into problems from time to time. In this section, we will go over how to diagnose and fix common issues such as **Wi-Fi connectivity problems**, **Bluetooth pairing issues**, and **screen freezes**.

Solving Wi-Fi, Bluetooth, and Connectivity Problems

Step 1: Troubleshooting Wi-Fi Connectivity

1. **Check Your Internet Connection**:

    o Verify that your **router** or **modem** is working by checking the **Wi-Fi** connection on another device.

    o If other devices are not connected, restart your **router** or **modem**.

2. **Restart Your Laptop**:

   o Sometimes, simply restarting your **Razer Blade 16** can resolve connectivity issues.

3. **Check Wi-Fi Settings**:

   o Go to **Settings** → **Network & Internet** → **Wi-Fi**.

   o Make sure **Wi-Fi** is turned on, and that your laptop is connected to the correct network.

4. **Forget and Reconnect**:

   o If you're still having trouble, **forget the network** and reconnect:

      ▪ Go to **Wi-Fi** settings, click on your network, and choose **Forget**.

      ▪ Reconnect by selecting the network and entering the **password**.

5. **Update Network Drivers**:

   o Open **Device Manager** (press **Win + X**, then select **Device Manager**).

   o Expand **Network adapters**, right-click on your **Wi-Fi driver**, and choose **Update driver**.

   o If there's no update, try uninstalling and reinstalling the driver.

Step 2: Troubleshooting Bluetooth Pairing Issues

1. **Ensure Bluetooth is On**:

   o Go to **Settings** → Devices → **Bluetooth & other devices**.

   o Ensure Bluetooth is **enabled** and your laptop is discoverable.

2. **Re-pair Your Devices**:

   o If your Bluetooth device is not connecting, try **removing** it from your Bluetooth list and then **re-pair** it by selecting **Add Bluetooth or other device** and following the pairing process.

3. **Update Bluetooth Drivers**:

   o In **Device Manager**, expand **Bluetooth**, right-click your Bluetooth adapter, and select **Update driver** to ensure you have the latest version.

Step 3: Troubleshooting Screen, Keyboard, or Trackpad Malfunctions

1. **For Screen Issues**:

   o Check the **brightness** by pressing the **Fn** key + **F7/F8** to adjust.

   o If the screen is **black**, press **Ctrl + Alt + Del** to check if it's a software crash or hardware issue.

   o Try connecting an external monitor to see if the issue is with the laptop's display.

2. **For Keyboard/Trackpad Issues**:

   o Ensure that the **keyboard and trackpad drivers** are up-to-date through **Device Manager**.

   o Check if the **trackpad** is disabled by pressing **Fn + F1** (or another key specific to your model) to toggle the trackpad on or off.

   o If the keys are not responding, you can **reset keyboard settings** by going to **Settings → Devices → Typing**.

Maintaining System Health

Maintaining your system is crucial for ensuring **long-term performance** and avoiding issues like **overheating** or **dust buildup**.

Cleaning and Maintaining Your Laptop to Prevent Dust and Overheating

1. **Regularly Clean Your Laptop**:

   o Use a **microfiber cloth** to clean the screen, keyboard, and trackpad.

   o **Compressed air** can be used to clean **vents** and **keyboard gaps**. Be careful not to blow dust **into** the vents but rather direct the air **out** of the laptop.

2. **Preventing Dust Buildup**:

- o **Place your laptop in a clean, dry environment** and avoid using it in dusty areas.

- o Use a **laptop cooling pad** to improve airflow and reduce the chance of overheating.

3. **Overheating Prevention**:

- o Ensure that the **cooling fans** are working properly by checking for abnormal noise or performance drops. If needed, clean the fan area with compressed air.

- o Keep your laptop on a **flat surface** to ensure good airflow. Avoid using it on soft surfaces like a bed or pillow.

Running Diagnostic Tools for Hardware and Software Health Checks

1. **Windows Memory Diagnostic Tool**:

- o Type **"Windows Memory Diagnostic"** in the search bar and click on the **app**.

- o Choose **Restart now and check for problems**. The system will restart and check your memory for errors. This is useful if you suspect issues with RAM.

2. **Check System Health with Built-in Tools**:

- o **Reliability Monitor**: Type **"Reliability Monitor"** in the search bar and open **View reliability history**. This tool can help you identify system crashes or issues.

- o **Event Viewer**: Type **"Event Viewer"** in the search bar, and navigate to **Windows Logs** → **System** for detailed error logs.

Software and Driver Updates

Ensuring that your **drivers** and **software** are up-to-date is essential for keeping your laptop running efficiently and securely.

How to Update Windows 11 and Razer Synapse for Optimal Performance

1. **Update Windows 11**:

   - o Go to **Settings** → **Windows Update** → **Check for updates**.

   - o If updates are available, install them to ensure you have the latest security patches and performance improvements.

2. **Update Razer Synapse**:

   - o Open **Razer Synapse**.

   - o Click on the **gear icon** in the upper-right corner to open **Settings**.

   - o Click **Check for Updates** to ensure you have the latest version of **Razer Synapse** for hardware control and performance optimization.

Updating GPU Drivers and System Software for the Latest Features

119

1. **Update GPU Drivers (NVIDIA)**:

    o Download and install the **GeForce Experience** software from **NVIDIA** if you haven't already.

    o Open **GeForce Experience**, sign in, and check for **driver updates** under the **Drivers** tab.

    o If updates are available, click **Download** and follow the installation instructions.

2. **Update System Drivers**:

    o Right-click the **Start Menu**, and select **Device Manager**.

    o Expand each category (e.g., **Display Adapters**, **Sound**), right-click the device, and select **Update Driver**.

Advanced Troubleshooting

For more advanced users, troubleshooting issues related to **performance bottlenecks**, **memory issues**, or **overclocking** settings is crucial for optimizing the system.

Using Built-in Diagnostic Tools (Windows Memory Diagnostic, Event Viewer)

1. **Windows Memory Diagnostic**:

    o As mentioned earlier, use **Windows Memory Diagnostic** to check for RAM issues.

2. **Event Viewer**:

- Use **Event Viewer** to view system logs for more detailed error information. This tool can help you identify recurring issues such as **system crashes** or **driver conflicts**.

Managing System Resource Usage and Identifying Performance Bottlenecks

1. **Task Manager**:

   - Press **Ctrl + Shift + Esc** to open **Task Manager**.

   - Go to the **Performance** tab to monitor CPU, memory, and disk usage.

   - If any resource is running at 100% usage, check the **Processes** tab to see what applications are using the most resources.

2. **Resource Monitor**:

   - Open **Resource Monitor** by typing **"resmon"** in the search bar.

   - This tool provides more detailed insight into CPU, disk, memory, and network usage. It can help identify which processes are causing bottlenecks.

Custom Overclocking and Tuning for Power Users

Overclocking can boost performance, but it needs to be done with caution.

1. **Enable Overclocking in BIOS**:

- o Reboot your laptop and press **F2** to enter the **BIOS** setup.

- o Look for **Performance** or **Overclocking** settings, and enable **CPU Overclocking** if desired. Be sure to **monitor temperatures** closely.

2. **Use Software to Overclock**:

- o Tools like **MSI Afterburner** allow you to adjust GPU settings for overclocking.

- o **Razer Synapse** also lets you tweak certain system performance settings for gaming.

3. **Monitor Temps**:

- o Always monitor the **temperature** of your CPU and GPU using tools like **HWMonitor** to avoid overheating when overclocking.

By following these troubleshooting and maintenance steps, you'll ensure your **Razer Blade 16** stays in top condition. From diagnosing Wi-Fi and Bluetooth issues to optimizing your system's performance through software updates and advanced troubleshooting tools, this guide provides a comprehensive approach to managing and maintaining your laptop. Whether you're dealing with **system crashes, performance slowdowns,** or **hardware malfunctions**, these steps will help you get back on track.

Appendices

Glossary of Terms

This section defines key terms related to your **Razer Blade 16** to help you understand the technical features and settings. Knowing these terms will allow you to get the most out of your laptop.

Key Terms and Definitions Related to the Razer Blade 16

- **CPU (Central Processing Unit)**: The primary processor responsible for running programs and tasks. The **Razer Blade 16** uses high-performance **Intel Core i9** processors for fast computing and multitasking.

- **GPU (Graphics Processing Unit)**: The component responsible for rendering images and video. The **Razer Blade 16** comes equipped with **NVIDIA GeForce RTX** graphics cards, ideal for gaming, video editing, and 3D rendering.

- **RAM (Random Access Memory)**: Temporary storage used by the CPU to store data for active applications. **Razer Blade 16** typically includes **16GB to 32GB DDR5 RAM** for smooth performance.

- **SSD (Solid State Drive)**: A fast storage device used to store the operating system and programs. The **Razer Blade 16** features a **1TB SSD**, providing fast boot times and quick data access.

- **Refresh Rate**: The number of times per second that the display updates the image. The **Razer Blade 16** has a **165Hz refresh rate**, ensuring smooth visuals in gaming and video playback.

- **Thunderbolt 4**: A high-speed connection standard that supports fast data transfer and external device connections. The **Razer Blade 16** supports **Thunderbolt 4** for connecting monitors, external GPUs, and other high-speed devices.

- **RGB Lighting**: Customizable **LED lighting** found on the keyboard and logo, which can be personalized through **Razer Synapse** for different colors and effects.

- **Overclocking**: Increasing the operating speed of the CPU or GPU beyond the manufacturer's specified limits to achieve higher performance. Overclocking may generate more heat, so it's important to monitor temperature levels.

- **Razer Synapse**: The software that allows you to customize your **Razer Blade 16**'s settings, including **RGB lighting**, **performance profiles**, and **macros**.

Razer Blade 16 Specifications

The **Razer Blade 16** is packed with high-end specifications that make it an excellent choice for both gaming and professional work. Below is a quick reference of its key features and specifications.

Full Specifications Reference for Quick Comparison

Component	Specification
Processor	Intel Core i9 (12th Gen) with up to 14 cores and 20 threads
Graphics Card	NVIDIA GeForce RTX 3060/3070/3080 (depending on configuration)
Display	16-inch Mini-LED with 2560 x 1600 resolution, 165Hz refresh rate, 100% DCI-P3 color gamut
RAM	16GB to 32GB DDR5
Storage	1TB SSD (Upgradeable)
Battery	80Wh, up to 8 hours of light use (depending on tasks)
Ports	1 x Thunderbolt 4, 2 x USB-A 3.2, 1 x HDMI 2.1, 1 x UHS-III SD card reader
Connectivity	Wi-Fi 6E, Bluetooth 5.2
Operating System	Windows 11 Home or Windows 11 Pro
Audio	Dolby Atmos for immersive sound
Weight	2.08 kg (4.59 lbs)
Dimensions	14.1 x 9.3 x 0.8 inches

Frequently Asked Questions (FAQ)

This section answers some of the most common questions users have when using the **Razer Blade 16**, as well as troubleshooting tips to resolve issues you may encounter.

Solutions to Common Issues and Troubleshooting Tips

1. **How do I improve my battery life?**

   o Enable **Battery Saver Mode** in **Windows 11** (Settings → System → Battery).

   o Lower the **screen brightness**, disable unnecessary background apps, and use **Power Saving** or **Balanced Mode**.

   o Disable **Wi-Fi** and **Bluetooth** when not in use.

2. **How do I update my drivers, especially for the GPU?**

   o Open **GeForce Experience** (if using NVIDIA) and go to the **Drivers** section to check for updates.

   o Alternatively, visit **Device Manager** → **Display Adapters**, right-click your GPU, and select **Update Driver**.

3. **What should I do if my screen freezes?**

- Try pressing **Ctrl + Alt + Del** and selecting **Task Manager** to end unresponsive programs.

- If the system is completely frozen, perform a **hard reset** by holding the power button for 10 seconds.

4. **My Bluetooth device won't connect. What should I do?**

- Ensure **Bluetooth** is enabled by going to **Settings** → **Devices** → **Bluetooth & other devices**.

- If it still doesn't work, try **removing** the device from the Bluetooth list and then **re-pair** it.

5. **How can I speed up my laptop?**

- Make sure your **SSD** has enough free space (delete unnecessary files or upgrade storage if needed).

- Run **Disk Cleanup** and **defragment** your drive. Disable unnecessary **startup programs**.

- Upgrade your **RAM** if possible, and ensure no **background processes** are consuming excessive system resources.

Keyboard Shortcuts and Customizations

Keyboard shortcuts and customizations can greatly enhance your productivity by allowing you to perform tasks faster and more efficiently. Here are some essential shortcuts and customization tips for your **Razer Blade 16**.

A List of Essential Shortcuts and Customization Options for Faster Use

Basic Keyboard Shortcuts:

- **Ctrl + C**: Copy
- **Ctrl + V**: Paste
- **Ctrl + X**: Cut
- **Ctrl + Z**: Undo
- **Ctrl + Y**: Redo
- **Alt + Tab**: Switch between open applications
- **Windows + D**: Show or hide the desktop
- **Windows + L**: Lock your laptop
- **Windows + E**: Open File Explorer

Razer Blade 16-Specific Shortcuts:

- **Fn + F7/F8**: Adjust screen brightness
- **Fn + F1/F2**: Enable or disable the **trackpad**.
- **Fn + F9**: Adjust **keyboard backlighting** (brightness and effects).

- **Fn + Spacebar**: Switch between **performance modes** (Balanced, Performance, Battery Saver).

Customizing Shortcuts Using Razer Synapse:

1. **Open Razer Synapse** and go to the **Keyboard** tab.

2. Select a **key** on the virtual keyboard that you want to **remap** or customize.

3. Assign a new function, such as launching an app, opening a website, or running a custom **macro**.

4. Use **Chroma** effects to customize key lighting and enhance the look of your keyboard for different activities (gaming, work, etc.).

Useful Resources

This section contains helpful resources for troubleshooting, getting support, and learning more about the **Razer Blade 16**.

Online Communities, Official Support, and Helpful Razer Resources

1. **Razer Official Support**:

   o Visit Razer's official **support page** for product manuals, FAQs, and troubleshooting guides.

2. **Razer Forums**:

   o Join the **Razer Insider** community to ask questions, share experiences, and interact with fellow Razer users and experts.

3. **Razer YouTube Channel**:

   o Visit Razer's official YouTube channel for tutorial videos, product reviews, and feature demonstrations.

4. **Razer Synapse Download**:

   o If you need to reinstall **Razer Synapse**, you can find the download on the official Razer website for full hardware customization.

5. **Razer Blade 16 Product Page**:

   o For up-to-date product information, configuration options, and the latest updates on the **Razer Blade 16**, refer to Razer's official product page.

This **appendices** section serves as your quick reference guide for essential terms, troubleshooting tips, keyboard shortcuts, and customization options. Whether you're looking for help with **Wi-Fi** connectivity issues, **keyboard** customization, or finding the right **software updates**, these resources will assist you in maximizing your **Razer Blade 16** experience.

Conclusion

As we wrap up this guide, let's take a moment to recap the **key features** of the **Razer Blade 16** and how you can make the most of them. Whether you're using it for gaming, creative work, or professional development, the **Razer Blade 16** offers an exceptional experience that will elevate your productivity and entertainment. Here's how you can make the most of your device and continue exploring the **Razer ecosystem.**

Recap of Key Features and How to Make the Most of the Razer Blade 16

The **Razer Blade 16** is designed to deliver outstanding performance with its **Intel Core i9 processor, NVIDIA GeForce RTX graphics,** and **Mini-LED display** with a **165Hz refresh rate.** This combination makes it an ideal choice for:

- **Gaming**: Enjoy ultra-smooth gameplay and stunning visuals thanks to the high-performance **GPU** and **high refresh rate** display.

- **Creative Work**: With up to **32GB of RAM** and **1TB of SSD storage**, the Blade 16 provides the power and speed needed for **video editing, 3D rendering,** and other creative tasks.

- **Professional Development**: Whether you're coding, developing, or running virtual machines, the **Razer Blade 16'**s processor and **high-performance RAM** will support all your needs.

To make the most of your Blade 16:

1. **Optimize Power Settings**: Switch between **Performance Mode** and **Battery Saver Mode** depending on your activity.

2. **Customize Settings with Razer Synapse**: Adjust **RGB lighting**, create **macros**, and tweak **performance profiles** for gaming or productivity.

3. **Keep Your System Clean**: Regularly clean your laptop, update drivers, and use built-in diagnostic tools to ensure smooth performance.

Exploring Advanced Usage: Gaming, Creative Work, Development, and More

The **Razer Blade 16** isn't just for general computing—it's designed to handle **advanced usage** scenarios:

- **Gaming**: With **NVIDIA RTX graphics** and **DLSS support**, you can enjoy immersive cloud gaming through **GeForce NOW** and **Xbox Cloud Gaming**, or run AAA games on **high settings** with smooth frame rates. Experiment with **performance profiles** and **overclocking** to push the limits.

- **Creative Work**: Whether you're a **photographer**, **video editor**, or **3D designer**, the **Mini-LED display** with **100% DCI-P3 color accuracy** and the **powerful GPU** allows you to work on high-end creative tasks with impressive precision. Use **Adobe Creative Suite** or **Autodesk Maya** for your creative projects.

- **Software Development**: From setting up **IDEs** (like **VSCode** and **JetBrains**) to working with

Docker containers and **Kubernetes** for cloud applications, the **Razer Blade 16** can handle all your development needs. The high-speed **Thunderbolt 4** ports allow you to connect to external devices such as **monitors**, **external storage**, or **GPUs** for maximum productivity.

- **Productivity**: Whether you're managing documents, spreadsheets, or collaborating with colleagues, the **Razer Blade 16** offers the performance to multitask efficiently. Utilize **Microsoft Office 365** or **Google Workspace** for seamless work-from-anywhere setups.

Continuing Your Journey with Razer Ecosystem Devices (Mice, Keyboards, etc.)

The **Razer Blade 16** is just the beginning of your experience with Razer's powerful ecosystem of devices. As you expand your setup, consider integrating **Razer peripherals** for a fully immersive and highly efficient environment.

- **Razer Mice**: Enhance your gaming or productivity with a **Razer mouse**. Whether you're into **FPS games** or **MMORPGs**, **Razer mice** feature **high-precision sensors** and customizable buttons that can be tailored to your exact needs.

- **Razer Keyboards**: Pair your **Blade 16** with a **Razer keyboard** for a fully customizable experience. **Razer Chroma RGB** allows you to sync your keyboard lighting with your game or workspace, creating a personalized ambiance.

- **Razer Headsets**: For the ultimate immersive experience in gaming or creative work, consider investing in a **Razer headset** with **Dolby Atmos** or **THX Spatial Audio** support. This will provide high-quality sound and microphone features for communication in multiplayer games or meetings.

- **Razer Accessories**: Other accessories like **Razer laptop stands, cooling pads**, and **external hard drives** will ensure you can extend your Blade 16's capabilities and maintain its optimal performance.

The **Razer Blade 16** offers cutting-edge performance in a compact, sleek design. By understanding and customizing its features, you can take full advantage of its power for **gaming, creative tasks, development**, and more. As you grow into the **Razer ecosystem**, your setup will continue to evolve, giving you all the tools you need to tackle any challenge with ease and style.

With this guide, you now have the knowledge to **optimize** your **Razer Blade 16** for your specific needs and maintain it for long-lasting performance. Enjoy your journey with one of the best laptops available, and embrace the full potential of the **Razer Blade 16** and its ecosystem.